SIX DOLLAR FAMILY

FROM SIX DOLLARS TO SIX FIGURES

Stacy Barr

Six Dollar Family

From Six Dollars to Six Figures

Stacy Barr

TABLE OF CONTENTS

Contents

INTRODUCTION

Money doesn't come easy to me. I grew up in a trailer built in the sixties with parents who were simple folk without much education. I wouldn't say we were "dirt" poor, but we were certainly not rolling in spare cash and catering to our every whim. We may not have had much and I may not have always been given the things that I wanted, but I never once went without anything that I needed. My mother was a stay at home mom who has had chronic health issues for most of my life. My father was the son of a laborer who worked low paying jobs for most of his life. Thus, I grew up watching my parents save in whatever little ways that they could. I am one-hundred percent sure that they didn't realize it, but watching them, I learned. Knowing how to live a thrifty or frugal lifestyle and putting those lessons into practice are two entirely different things though and in fact, I can honestly say that for the most part, I did the exact opposite of what my father had taught me.

Flash forward about 15 years or so to 2010 when I very suddenly found myself a 27-year-old homeless mom with a 5-year-old daughter. This book is called "The Six Dollar Family" because that's what we were the day that she and I entered that homeless shelter that we would spend most the year in. We were a family with exactly six dollars to our name.

In 2011, I started the blog that would eventually also become known as Six Dollar Family (sixdollarfamily.com) and our lives would never be the same again. It was called something different back then, but finally I began to apply those things that I had picked up from my Dad and things (finally) began to move in the right direction for us. Fast forward 5 years and we have almost reached our goals as a family. My once little coupon blog has grown beyond what I ever intended or expected it to be and now we extend that one step further with the Six Dollar Family book.

This book should an extension of my blog. It's the stuff I've always meant to put in a post, but at the time of this writing haven't gotten around to. I have completely rebuilt not only my life, but my daughter's as well using the tips in this book. I have expanded on the strong foundation that my childhood gave me by continuing to learn and I will reach the goals that I set for myself and my family in a much shorter time frame than I initially thought.

If you are struggling with your budget, if you're finding it hard to make ends meet, if you know there is a better way to live, but just can't see it; this book is for you. I have been where you are, I have struggled the same way and I have fought the same fights. I speak from many failed attempts and personal experience when I say that things can get better. It just takes a little bit of work and of course, one big fighting attitude. Even if you're a veteran saver, I'm sure you'll find something useful within these pages.

No, my family isn't a six-figure family yet, but we are well on our way. The methods in this book have worked for us and I'm positive they will for you as well. Whether you read it all the way through or just cherry pick certain parts, it is my sincere hope that I can help you too become a six-figure family.

Thank you for picking up this book and giving it a chance. I don't know if I'll be able to help you, but that is my hope. If I can help even one person with the writings in these pages and with those on my blog, it will have all been worth it.

Stacy

How to Use This Book To Save

This book is broken down in a very simple way. The front of the book focuses on budgeting, the middle on saving and cutting your expenses and the end about keeping on the road to building the six-figure future that you're looking for.

For some, the tips on budgeting will be too elementary and just a re-hash of information they already know. For others, it will be an eye-opening experience with new information they have never seen before. The same could be said for the rest of the book.

Use this book however you need to. If a specific chapter is already familiar to you and you feel there is absolutely nothing else that you can learn on that subject? Skip it. If a tip is something you already do? Consider yourself wise and move on.

My personal advice though is to read the entire thing front to back even if there are topics that you are already strong in. It never hurts to have a refresher and as the old saying goes, *"you learn something new every day."*

Why Only Six Figures? Why Not Seven?

Please understand that I don't mean to discourage you from building your savings and investments beyond six figures. However, when doing the research for this book, I discovered that a lot of people seem to think that seven figures is unattainable and were intimidated by the idea of trying to go from literally nothing to millions. In truth, that couldn't be farther from the truth, but if six figures is easier for most to swallow? Six figures is what we will work on.

By all means, build your accounts to seven, eight or nine figures. Take the advice that you find here and that you get from other financial whiz kids who are much smarter than I am and run with it. Don't let the number of zero's scare you and instead, let it motivate you.

ARE YOU REALLY FRUGAL?

The other day I was having a conversation with a very close friend when she made some offhanded comment about how she had thought she was frugal, but after talking with me, she then realized that she wasn't. This friend of mine does what she can to save, but she's not the type to go out and seek a new way to save. She's more of the *"if I save, I save and if not, then not"* school of thought. Frugality is a lifestyle. It isn't about saving a few dollars each shopping trip or about finding the occasional deal. It's about saving as much money as possible, in every aspect of your life.

DEFINING FRUGAL

Frugality is commonly defined as saving, but it also means being a wise saver. Anyone can save, but to be truly frugal you also must be wise about it. Without a smart way of thinking and wise decision making, you will run the risk of falling into the trap of thinking that you're doing your best when you may not be. That trap is wide and it is deep and once you're there, it can take years to climb out of.

Whenever I mention anything frugal in general in this book, read it while keeping the definition of frugal, "wise saver," in mind.

FRUGAL VS. THRIFTY

Most people have a basic idea of what the words frugal and thrifty mean to them, however, they can be vastly different for each person. What one person considers to be simply frugal, another might see as being a cheapskate and over the line for their family.

No matter what your personal thoughts on what they mean are, there are a few common themes for both that seem to hold true for most everyone I've spoken with.

CHARACTERISTICS OF A THRIFTY PERSON

The thrifty person may look for a deal on an item they need or want, but rarely waits for **the** deal. Instead, they are perfectly fine with not saving at all and will even pay retail if needed.

The thrifty person may know what tomorrow's dinner is, but they don't plan their meals or their grocery shopping. Instead, the often wing it with boxed or prepackaged meals they picked up on sale, wander through the store buying what "looks good" and often give into wasteful impulse buys.

The thrifty person may have a budget, but it isn't their go to before they spend money. In fact, they may not even update it regularly and often find themselves over budget on a regular basis.

The thrifty person easily confuses need versus want and they're perfectly willing to go into deep debt to obtain their want if the deal "looks" good to them.

A thrifty person makes the minimum payments on their debt and sometimes will even skip a payment or two.

A thrifty person may have a few dollars in savings, but does not have a dedicated emergency fund.

A thrifty person uses coupons, but often doesn't use them in a way that maximizes their savings.

A thrifty person just accepts their bank account as gospel truth. They are wishers who "wish" they could "be rich" and wish they could save more, but they will never take real initiative to figure out how to do both things.

CHARACTERISTICS OF A FRUGAL PERSON

A frugal person will wait when they need or want something until they find *the* deal; even if it means waiting weeks or months.

A frugal person menu plans regularly using what they already have in their home first and grocery shopping second. They often cook meals from scratch and know the "true" cost of boxed meals doesn't always mean just a monetary value.

A frugal person tracks their budget and their expenses weekly (at a minimum) so that they know where their money is going.

A frugal person understands what their needs are and can tell the difference between a true need and a want. They understand that debt is never the answer to a want and even for a need, it is the absolute last option.

A frugal person pays off any debts as quickly as possible and understands why doing so is important.

A frugal person has a separate emergency fund set aside and puts money into it on a regular basis preparing themselves for any emergency that may arise.

A frugal person shops using coupons, sales, savings apps or websites, and know the price per unit/ounce of everything they buy to save the most and what their maximum price per unit is.

A frugal person (or "wise saver") understands that their bank account balance directly correlates with the amount of work they put into it. They do what they need to do to see that dollar amount grow and usually have much more money than they may seem to have.

As you can see, there are a few significant characteristics that stick with each "type" of person. Obviously frugal minded people are generally bigger savers with lower costs of living and they generally have larger bank balances too. We'll talk about why later, but I want you to understand. No matter which one you fall into...there is always room for improvement.

DEFINING YOUR FRUGAL & YOUR WHY

As I said in the beginning of this chapter, each person or family will define frugal living differently. For your family to succeed, you need to have a good basic idea of what it means to you. Living a frugal lifestyle usually means making cuts and sacrifices in places that you wouldn't normally chose to. If you don't have that line clearly laid out for yourself, it can be extremely easy to lose sight of where it lies and why you're living as cheaply as possible.

Your reasons for wanting to save are different from anyone else's too. You may be trying to cut costs due to lost income, you may be trying to plan for your retirement, you may be trying to purchase your first home or you may just be playing a game to see how low you can go. Whatever your reasons are, make certain that they're always in the forefront of your mind. Keeping them in mind will give you the motivation that you need when saving money gets tough (and it will).

MIND YOUR THOUGHTS

As I was reading the reviews for the original version of this book, I came across one that stated that the thoughts and ideas given within were "too much work for a few pennies." While it's true that not every single tip will help you save thousands, I wanted to address that single review right here in the revised version of the book itself.

Frugality isn't meant to be a hit or miss, take it when you want it and leave it when you don't. It's meant to be a lifestyle. Yes, there are things that a frugal person will do that only save a few pennies a month, but the thing is? Pennies very quickly add up to dollars and dollars add up to six figures.

If you go through life looking at your finances with your mind set on the fact that things will a.) Never get better, b.) That it's not worth trying to save or c.) That you only want to save big bucks? You're going to find yourself facing financial ruin quicker than you might think.

Negative thoughts, such as the one above, are the simplest way to destroy your financial future. They are the kind of thoughts that lead you to believe it is okay to buy that big-ticket item when you know that you have a bill due. They are the kind of thoughts that whisper loudly that the vacation you're planning is much more important than paying off your student loans. They are the kind of thoughts that lead to impulsive decisions and eventually financial ruin if you give into them too many times. Instead, focus on the good that your savings, even pennies and nickels, will do for you and your family.

The Basic Budget

By now in your life, you probably already know that every household should have a budget, however, there is a very big difference between knowing that you should have one and having one and there is a very big difference between having a budget and following it. It absolutely amazes me how many families live without a budget! Usually those families are the ones that are struggling each month because they're not taking a few minutes each month or week to create a plan for their family. Creating your budget is the easy part. Sticking to it is an entirely different ball game!

The point of having a budget is to ensure that you are totally in control of your money. You work hard for your money, but your money shouldn't control you or your life and when you're living without a budget that is exactly what happens. Creating a budget and using a budget will allow you to control it instead of the other way around.

There are several different types of budgets that you can use, but the key to success in picking one is to find one that works for you and your household. Many people try to run several types of budgets at one time or to use a budget that doesn't work for them, but doing that only causes chaos and more trouble than not having a budget at all.

When you run multiple household budgets at once, it's hard to keep track of what money is coming in and what money is going out. Running more than one budget can also be very overwhelming and because of that, you'll end up bleeding money and you're likely to give up very quickly.

I can recall very vividly an incident that happened with my own budget a few years back. First, I need to admit that I am a budget software snob. I have very specific things that I am looking for in my budget and if those things are not available in a software, I will move on. What happened a couple of years ago was a result of this snobbery and it wasn't too long before we were in trouble. I came across a budgeting software that I kind of liked. It didn't have everything I was looking for, but did offer most of it so we started using it as a test run. Before long I found another software that I wanted to try and eventually a third. We switched budget software option and budget types three times that month.

I can tell you that it wasn't too terribly long before my budget and finances were completely off track and sideways. I had confused not only myself, but my husband as well by playing hopscotch with our finances. We ended up with several past due bills to play catch up on and I learned a valuable lesson.

Find a budget system that works and stick with it.

Remember it can take several months and lots of trial, error, heartbreak and tears to get the hang of budgeting. **You will fail at it the first time or two. You will go over budget. You may even end up totally broke while you're learning.** That's okay though! Don't give up too soon! It's all part of the process and soon enough, you'll be budgeting like a pro!

One last thing, give your budget the time that it needs each month. Rushing through it will only hurt you since you're more likely to make mistakes when you're in a hurry. Budgets are basic math at their core and while you may be secure in your ability to add or subtract, we all make mistakes when we're in a hurry. My own budget takes around two hours each month (total), but can take a lot longer if I'm cracking down on things or if things are not adding up the way they should be. Instead, I give my budget the amount of time that it requires and because I don't hurry things along, I rarely have an issue with miscalculations or incorrect estimates.

TRACKING YOUR EXPENSES

I know. Really, I do. Every single personal finance or frugal living blog, book or guru out there is telling you to track your expenses. Have you wondered why?

Because it is so very important to do!

Aside from the obvious reasons; seeing where your money is going, making sure you're not over budget in a certain category, making sure you have enough income, etc; there are a plethora of other reasons that you need to be doing this.

I once had a blog reader email me for help making extra money. Her husband had a gambling addiction and had drained their accounts dry. She had suddenly found her family in a situation where they stood to lose their home, their utilities were being shut off, the car was repossessed and she had no real idea why. When I started asking questions, I soon found that while they had a budget, they were not actively tracking their expenses. In fact, they weren't tracking them at all.

This one simple action could have saved their finances.

Had she been paying attention to their bank accounts and debit cards, she would have had a better chance of catching her husband's gambling withdraws. Instead, she found herself facing a financial disaster like she had never known or expected before.

Tracking your expenses is incredibly simple. Pick up a small notebook or account ledger and keep it and a pen on you anytime you're likely to spend money. When you do spend something, write it down. Eventually, you'll start to see a clear pattern of where your money is going and where you need to cut back.

If you use a budgeting software like Mint.com, it will track your expenses for you if you have your bank account connected. This is a great option for people who have a short memory and can easily forget to write things down.

For families that often have two people spending money, it can be helpful to track in multiple places. My husband and I both spend money, but we're not always together when we do. Most of the money that I spend is online for business expenses or our daughters homeschool items. For this reason, he carries two checkbook registers (one for each bank account that we have debit cards for) and I also keep an account ledger book at my desk. When I spend money, or get a deposit, I write that in the account ledger. When he spends money, he uses his checkbook registers. At the end of the week, we sit down together and put all the transactions into a third account ledger that tracks our bank accounts to make sure they match what the bank says.

It is this very simple action each week that keeps our bank accounts and our budgets on track.

TYPES OF BUDGETS

I could write an entire book solely on the topic of different budgets, but really, who wants to read that? Instead, I want to look at the three most common methods of budgeting. Budgets are extremely personal. What works for me may not work for you and vice versa. Chances are, one of these three will work for you, but you won't know until you try them on for size. Whichever one you choose, make sure that you give yourself time to learn your system and to adapt to it. What you'll likely see happen is over time, you'll start tweaking it until it fits your family perfectly.

LINE ITEM BUDGET

Using a line item budget is a great option for those who love working with spreadsheets and who have a little bit of extra money to play with in their bank accounts since most amounts are estimated. If you don't fit both of those though, this may not be the best option for you and your family.

The way the line item budget works is every line gets a name with an estimated amount. The hope and goal are to stay under the estimated amount. If you are planning the next month's budget and you know your electric bill is normally $100 then that is the amount you will estimate. Once the bill comes in you will write the exact amount you paid.

At the end of the month, total up your expenses and estimates, see how close you were and adjust the new month's budget to fit any over budgets or under budgets that you may have had.

Once you use this budget for a few months your estimates will get more accurate and you will be in better control of your money, but do keep in mind that at first, they may be off; especially if you're not currently actively tracking your expenses.

This is the type of budget that we personally use. For me, I find it gives me better control over where my money is going and where it's not going. Not a penny leaves my pocket without me knowing it. The difference between what I do and writing down your actual payment is that I purposely over estimate on things like utilities and then I pay that amount. As a result, I have 3 months' worth of credits built up for most of my regular monthly expenses. If I suddenly have a bad month, I'm covered in those areas without having to stress that my payment will be late or completely missed.

THE ENVELOPE SYSTEM BUDGET

The envelope budget is very easy to use and works great for people who deal mainly in cash. The first thing you will need to do is determine how much money you have coming in as income every month. This is especially important if your income is irregular (meaning that you don't make the same amount week after week.). Then, you'll need to make a list that includes all your expenses.

Do not cheat in this area! Make sure to write down all your expenses, no matter how small they might seem. If you spend a dollar every morning on coffee write down thirty dollars for coffee every month. These expenses become your budget categories.

Once you have all your income and expenses listed, gather up some envelopes. They don't need to be fancy. Plain ol' regular envelopes will work, but if you want reusable ones, a quick search on Amazon will bring up some very nice ones. On each envelope, you will write down your budget categories and the amount you have budgeted for it.

Example: Groceries $300

Create an envelope for each category and fill each envelope with the amount of cash that you budgeted for it. When you go grocery shopping, take your grocery envelope with you and only spend money from that specific envelope. If you go over your budget, you must put items back. At the end of the month take each envelope and see if you have any left-over money inside. If you do, redistribute it for the next month or put it into savings.

One final word on the envelope system, do **not** remove money from envelope to envelope. If you're over budget, you're over budget for that category this month. Make sure to budget more money in that category next month.

Percentage Budget

A percentage budget is great for people who love math and like exact numbers. Some people will argue that this budget is the hardest to get accurate, but for the people that use it on a regular basis, it's an awesome way to make sure everything is accounted for.

With the percentage budget, you start off with 100% (your take home income) and from there every expense gets a percentage. Gas might get 5% of your income and groceries 10%. You do this with each expense category and you should end up with 0%. Try to end up with 0% left...even if it means sticking a ton in savings and that is never a bad thing.

THE "IN CASE I FORGOT" BUDGET CATEGORY

My husband laughs at me often over this, but it is truly something that I feel every budget should have. Most of us have a handful of expenses that are easily forgotten. While they may be smaller expenses, they could cause major damage to your budget if they aren't accounted for. To cover these expenses, I keep an "in case I forgot" budget category. It is a solid $100 in my budget every month. While I might not use that money each month, I'm still covered if I need it.

YOUR EMERGENCY FUND

As soon as possible, be sure to set aside money for an emergency fund and then don't touch it. Ideally, your emergency fund should contain enough money to cover three to six months of expenses but if you can't do that comfortably, one-thousand dollars is what is usually recommended. I personally think that for people who are having it rough right now, $1,000 is a hard number to get to. For those families, I recommend $500 to start, building up to a larger amount as you get your finances under control.

Having one in place though is one of the most important things you can do for your family financially no matter what your current financial situation is. If you've got an emergency fund set up, you will be prepared to cover anything unexpected that life may throw your way.

Make sure that you aren't keeping your emergency fund at home in cash. It's way too easy to accidentally spend it. Keep it in a bank. Your local bank is a good place to start but if you don't have a local bank, there are quite a few online only banking options that are just as good.

BUILDING YOUR FUND EASILY

One of the easiest ways to build your fund is to throw any money you have left at the end of the month into your fund, but that can take longer than what most people are comfortable with.

If you're in that crowd and want to build it up faster, you could take a second job, sell items that you no longer want, or use a spare change system to quickly add money to the account. When we were rebuilding ours after having to use it on a pop up expense, I sold clothes at an online consignment shop, picked up freelance writing work and even took jobs working for other bloggers to get it funded again quickly. In the end, I kept those other jobs because I like having the extra money to add to our savings at the end of each month.

If you're feeling discouraged that your fund just isn't building as quickly as you'd like, take a short breather. You're not going to do any good by being overwhelmed and stressed. I know that at times it can seem like this mountain is too high to climb, but chances are you'll find that once you get the ball rolling? It rolls very quickly.

SPARE CHANGE CHALLENGE

Confused as to what a spare change challenge is? Exactly what it sounds like! At the end of each day, dump your spare change (actual change and any change balances in your bank accounts) into your savings. I know it may only be a few cents, but you will be shocked at how quickly those pennies turn into dollars. Want to make it grow quicker? Do it with one dollar or five dollar bills! It will grow by leaps and bounds then! I've even seen a few (*brave*) souls do it with twenties!

One way that you might consider for adding to your savings is to use a micro-saver or micro-investor such as Digit. These sites analyze your spending and pull small amounts out of your checking account automatically. They work for helping to build your emergency fund because the amounts are so small that you never miss the money. I personally use Digit and love it. I save without even realizing it and have honestly been shocked at how much quickly it has padded our fund!

A WORD OF CAUTION ON MICRO-SAVERS

As with anything that you're giving access to your money, be sure that the micro-investor or micro-saver that you're using is FDIC insured. Having that insurance takes protecting your wealth one step further.

TAKE A SIDE JOB

If you don't have enough wiggle room in your budget to easily and quickly stash funds away, taking a side job is the only way to build your emergency fund. Your side job doesn't need to be overly complicated and in all honesty, it is probably best that it isn't. You can do quick things such as mowing lawns, cleaning homes or baby-sitting to rack up the spare cash that you need for your emergency fund.

WHEN TO USE YOUR EMERGENCY FUND

Once you've got your emergency fund fully built, you'll need to practice some discretion as to when you use it. Set a few rules for yourself and for your fund and stick to them. Guard that money carefully and when you need it, it will be there for you.

IN CASE OF EMERGENCY

As the name of this section implies, your fund is for emergencies, but what makes up an emergency can be different for different people and families. For most families, this will include things like emergency car repairs, emergency medical expenses, loss of income, unexpected legal expenses, and other big ticket expenses you might not otherwise be able to cover.

No matter what your personal emergency is, make absolute certain that if you're using your emergency fund that it is a true emergency. I'm sorry to tell you this, but karate class isn't an emergency. Christmas gifts are not an emergency. Your car breaking down is. Covering your utilities after the loss of a job is a true emergency. A flight home after a death in the family is a true emergency. Knowing the difference and guarding your emergency fund so that you are only using it for what it is intended for is one of the best financial steps you can take for yourself.

One of the biggest mistakes that I have seen my blog readers make is that they are using their emergency funds when it isn't a true emergency. You are setting those funds aside for when you really and truly need them. If you use them ahead of time, they won't be there when you do need to rely on them.

SAVE ON YOUR GROCERIES

Have you ever heard the saying, "not enough money for the month?" I have and in fact, I've used it myself in the past more than I care to admit. I'm sure that we all have at one time or another. One of the best ways to help relieve that "more month than money" issue is to lower your grocery bill. Groceries are often one of the largest expenses that most of us have so it makes sense for us to start the "how to save" part of this book there. There's absolutely no reason for any family to be spending four hundred dollars or more per month on groceries, even if you have a large family. You can still feed your family nutritious and tasty meals on a budget with just a little bit of work.

KNOW YOUR UNIT PRICE

Every single item that you buy has a unit price. Some will be in pounds, others in ounces and a few will be random. Knowing your price per unit will give you the tools you need to figure out whether the price is a true deal or whether it's something that you can save more on at another store.

Knowing the cost per unit of what you're buying helps you to set up a top-line price point. This price point is the absolute most that you are willing to pay for that item. For instance, the absolute most that I will pay for a roll of bathroom tissue is $0.16 per single roll. Why? Because I know that I can almost always find a sale or deal to get it at that price or cheaper. Once you've set your price points for the things your family uses on a regular basis, stick to them and stock up once you find an item that meets it.

Figuring out the cost per unit of an item is quite simple, but it's not a common practice for a very large percentage of shoppers. To figure it out, you simply take the cost of your item and divide it by the quantity of the product.

For example, if you were looking for the cost per unit on a 24-count package of bath tissue that is priced at $3.99, you would divide $3.99 by 24. In this case your cost per unit would be $0.166 or $0.17 per roll after rounding up.

Another example is a 144-load bottle of laundry detergent priced at $8.99. $8.99 divided by 144 equals $0.062 or $0.06 per load when rounded down.

STRETCH A MEAL

Stretching a meal is a great way to cut down on the amount of food that your family is eating and it does it in a way that doesn't take away from them. Pasta, beans and rice are two of the cheapest foods that you can buy. With coupons, you can usually get them close to free and even without coupons they're not that expensive. They also make great meal fillers. Instead of fixing a double portion of something or using the full amount of called for in a recipe, add a cup or so of pasta, beans or rice. Your meal will seem larger; portions will be more filing and you won't be spending quite as much as you would if you cooked double or used the recipe like normal.

This works well with soups and casseroles, but things like burgers can be easily stretched as well.

Toss the Boxes

Homemade is always best and while I'm sure you've heard it before, making things homemade instead of eating boxed mixes and kits, is best. Not only is homemade better for your health, but it's usually cheaper as well. Learning things like how to make your own bread ($0.44 per loaf on average) or how to make your own mayo ($0.15 per cup) will not only have your family raving about the taste, but you'll be jumping for joy that you're not spending as much to feed them. If your cooking skills need to be brushed up on, there are plenty of free cooking classes and free baking classes online that you could take.

Another plus side to cooking from scratch? You'll eat out a lot less. Home cooked food just tastes better and once you've gotten used to it? Restaurant food will pale in comparison.

In 2014, my own family went through significant financial issues due to a loss of income. One of the best things that we did that year was to stop buying as much as we possibly could and to start making what we could. Now, we are at a point where we make over 60 items ourselves each month. The amount of money that we have saved by doing so is huge. I honestly think that it has been a large enough savings to say that we would not have made it through 2014 intact if it hadn't been for that savings.

Plan Your Dinners

Aside from knowing the cost per unit and making more homemade meals, menu planning is the biggest way that you can save on your food bill, help you be more organized and just generally reduce the number of "what's for dinner" questions that are asked in your home. When you're planning your menu, you use what you have on hand first and shop second meaning you're wasting less and are in the store for a smaller amount of time. Both will help you save big in the long run. If you're new to it, planning a menu that you will feed their family can be incredibly intimidating. If you're one of these people, don't be because when it boils down to it, planning your family's menu is quite simple.

Some plan by date and meal while others simply plan for 30 meals and leave the dates up in the air. Some plan for breakfast, lunch and dinner and others only plan dinners. You don't have to be rigid with it if you don't want to or if that won't work for you. I personally leave my dates open and only plan dinners. Once a week I go to my monthly menu and choose what we're eating for the upcoming week. I like having the ability to choose what we're having for dinner based on what everyone is wanting to eat that week. For lunch, we usually eat left overs and breakfasts are up to each person with the choices being whatever cereal we have on hand, eggs, or oatmeal.

6 STEPS TO A PLANNED MENU

1. Make a list of your family's favorite recipes.
2. Take a pantry, refrigerator and freezer inventory.
3. Match as many recipes as you can to the items you have on hand.
4. Use a calendar to plan 30 meals from the recipes you chose. A good idea for this step is to plan for 15 different meals, eaten twice a month.
5. Grocery shop for the items that you don't have on hand, but need to make recipes you'd like to have on your menu. Buy nothing that isn't on your list.
6. Cook dinner per your menu plan!

That was easy, wasn't it? Once your menu is planned, stick to it. It isn't going to help you save anything if you make it and then forget about it.

A WORD ABOUT FREEZER COOKING

Freezer cooking used to be considered something that only the most frugal and "cheap" people did and those who practiced it were occasionally looked at as odd or strange. These days though, freezer cooking has become mainstream and the practice is recommended just about everywhere you look. We have been freezer cooking for well over 10 years now and I tell you this from many years of both success and failure:

Freezer cooking can make *or* break not only your grocery budget, but your time management schedule as well.

When you plan for a freezer cooking session, you will be buying the groceries need in bulk, spending hours prepping food and using precious freezer space. This means that while it can give you a *huge* savings on your grocery bill, it can also kill that same grocery budget.

If you do not have the time to freezer cook, don't attempt to. If you aren't going to follow through with your freezer cooking session, don't buy the items needed. If the food is only going to go to waste, give it up. You will be doing nothing more than wasting your grocery money for the month and potentially putting your family in a tight spot.

However, if you can devote a day or three to fixing meals for a month or more, if you will cut up those peppers, dice the onions and brown the meat, if you will get things cooked before they go bad, then by all means, get your freezer cooking on.

If you can't devote the time to freezer cooking, you can still work on filling your freezer. Cook a double meal when you make your dinner. Serve half and freeze the other half. Your freezer will fill more slowly, but you will not be wasting money on a session gone bad.

When done correctly, freezer cooking can be a great way to save both time and money, but please be very careful. I have seen too many families not have groceries for the month because of a freezer cooking session gone bad.

Combo Savings

Have you ever looked at your sale flyers and noticed that a lot of grocery stores are offering combo deals? If not, check your local grocery stores the next time that you're preparing to grocery stop. These combo deals can be hit or miss, but most the time they can be used to significantly lower the cost of a meal or two.

Most of them are a buy one get a few specific items free, but occasionally you can find them with different requirements. Just be sure that you read the deal fully and figure out your cost per unit before you buy.

Meat Combos

Another popular combo that I'm seeing stores carry more often are combination meat packages. They are usually a combo of ground beef, chicken or pork, but I've found them at my stores in Texas with steak in them as well. Depending on the size of your family, you can rack up some significant savings with them, but if you have a large family, you'll want to look at the cost per meal. They typically don't have a large amount of any one specific meat in them so a larger family may end up paying more if they buy them.

At my local store, I can pick one of these packages up for around twenty dollars. That gets me around three pounds of ground beef, six to eight pork chops and either one meal of steak or one meal of chicken depending on which package I grab. Since we're a family of three, I can pick up meat for six to seven meals for under $20.00.

By contrast, my best friend has a family of six. In her case, she would pay $20.00 for what would amount to two or three meals. The combo packages are a great deal for my family, but a bad deal for hers.

USE GIFT CARD SPECIALS TO YOUR ADVANTAGE

Gift card deals aren't hard to find and buy using them to your advantage, you can cut your grocery spending some. If you buy gift cards for stores you shop on a regular basis, you'll slowly start to see the savings add up. If you're paying forty dollars for a fifty dollar Kroger gift card, you're saving ten dollars on fifty dollars' worth of groceries. Even if you only did this once a month, you would still save one-hundred twenty dollars a year on your grocery bill.

One of my absolute favorite places to get discount gift cards from is Raise. I like that I can save a few bucks here and there and that I can get them for not only places like Walmart and Target, but also that I can pick them up for places that I buy gifts from. I may only be saving a few bucks each time, but that savings adds up considerably over time.

MAKE CLEARANCE BUYS YOUR FRIEND

My husband knows that when I hit the meat section of the store, I am looking for one thing; clearance stickers. Recently I bought two pieces of pork loin for over sixty percent what they were at full price. There is nothing wrong with them, they're still in date and I saved just by walking a little further down the aisle from the full priced ones. Why were they marked down? They were odd cuts and the store felt that they wouldn't sell as well as the others.

In some stores, you'll need to look hard to find marked down meat. I've seen it in several places, but far corners of meat coolers seem to be a pretty common place. For other stores, they'll put the marked down meat in with the full priced meat so that it is easier to find. Some stores even have a specific time of day that they mark meat down. It will all just depend on your store so be sure to keep your eyes open.

Also, never be afraid to ask for a markdown. Most stores have rules that state that meat must be pulled from the coolers early in the day that it expires. If you find one that expires today, take it to the meat counter and ask them if they will mark it down since it will expire soon. In a lot of cases, you'll find that they'd rather sell it than toss it and this can mean big savings for you. Some of my long-time blog readers might remember when I posted about "Edgar the Super Chicken." Edgar was a whole roasting chicken that I saved almost 70% on because he was about to go out of date. Why was Edgar a super chicken? Because he saved me 70%! Sure, you might be told no when you ask, but you might also save big. You'll never know until you try.

SAVE IN YOUR HOME

Aside from the cost of groceries, household costs are often the place that a lot of budgets get off track. I'm not talking about utilities either. I'm talking pure household costs. Things like cleaning supplies, appliances and furniture can all cost you an arm and leg over time, but they don't have to. If you're careful, you can keep those costs down and maybe even save a buck or two in the process.

CLEAN LIKE GRANDMA DID

Most cleaners today are not only full of toxic chemicals that are not only horrid for your family, but they're also ridiculously overpriced. You can clean your entire home for less than ten dollars a month using nothing but lemon, salt, vinegar and baking soda and that includes laundry soap.

MAKE YOUR OWN LAUNDRY DETERGENT

Homemade powdered laundry soap is incredibly easy to make and cleans better than the commercial stuff. Take ¼ cup Borax, 1 cup Arm & Hammer Washing Soda and 1/3 bar Ivory soap, Zote or Fels Naptha. Grate the bar of soap and mix well with the other 2 ingredients. Use 2-3 tablespoons for the average load of laundry (more if it's heavily soiled)

"DIY" Fabric Softener

Want to ditch commercial liquid fabric softener? Use ¼ cup of vinegar instead. It does the job just as well with a much lower cost.

If you currently use dryer sheets and want to continue, I have a great tutorial on how to make your own homemade reusable dryer sheets on the Six Dollar Family blog. These are the ones that we use in our own home and they've quickly become a favorite of our readers.

You will need:

- old t-shirt
- Mason Jar with lid
- 3/4 cup vinegar
- 1/4 cup water
- Essential Oils for Fragrance – I like to use Lemon or Orange oils.

Cut your t-shirt into squares that are about 6x6" in size. Add the water, vinegar and essential oils to your mason jar then stuff the t-shirt pieces in. You may have to work to get them all in but they should all fit.

Don't worry if they aren't all wet at first. They will all soak up the liquid. Use like a regular dryer sheet in your dryer then set aside for your next batch once they're dry.

Homemade Dishwasher Soap

If you have a dishwasher, make sure you do two things. One, only run it in the evening when the power is cheaper and two, make your own liquid dishwasher soap. We used to use the tablets, but stopped once we tried a homemade version. Our homemade version cleans better and it's so much cheaper per load than the tablets or powdered stuff at the store.

You Will Need:

- 2 Tbsp. lemon juice
- ¾ cup Super-Washing Soda
- ½ cup Borax
- ¼ cup liquid unscented Castile soap
- 4 cups water
- Essential Oils (I like using NOW brand Lemon Essential Oil)

Place water in a large heavy bottomed pot and heat on medium-high heat until boiling. Stir in super washing soda and stir until dissolved. Then reduce the heat, add the Borax and stir until it is dissolved well. Simmer on low for 20 minutes making sure that you stir it with a whisk often. Be sure that you use a whisk too to help break up any lumps of powder that might form. I've never had that happen but I suppose it could.

Remove from heat and allow to cool completely. Its best to let it cool overnight so be sure to sit it in an area where it won't be disturbed. Once mixture has cooled and sat overnight, it should have a gel consistency. If you're using essential oils to give it a cleaning or scent boost, add them now then give it a good stir again to combine and transfer to a quart mason jar.

To use: Add 1-2 Tbsp. of detergent to each load of dishes in the soap compartment of your dishwasher.

HOMEMADE ALL-PURPOSE CLEANER

Want an awesome all-purpose cleaner? It's extremely simple to make and works for cleaning, degreasing and disinfecting. You can even use it on hard wood floors and laminate.

Take orange peels and add them to a pint-sized mason jar. Fill the jar with white vinegar and screw a lid and ring on. Let it sit for 7-10 days.

After the oil from the oranges has infused the vinegar, pour into a spray bottle making sure that you strain it through cheesecloth or a coffee filter first. Top your spray bottle off with water and use like any other cleaner.

HOMEMADE SCRUBBING PASTE

Skip the harsh chemical pastes and instead mix baking soda and table salt with enough water to make a thick paste. Spread on the area that you need to scrub and scrub away. It will clean every bit as well as the store-bought stuff for a considerably cheaper price.

Keep Your Appliances Maintained

Have you priced new appliances lately? If not, you might be surprised at just how expensive they are. When we moved into the house we currently live in from an apartment, we needed to buy a fridge and washer/dryer set. I bought new and forked out over fifteen hundred dollars for the three very basic appliances. For such big-ticket items, you need to be sure they are in good working order so that you don't end up having to replace them before their time. If you're constantly replacing them, you'll end up wasting an entire boatload of money.

For your fridge, make sure that you're pulling it away from the wall and cleaning the coils at least every 3 months. Ideally, you should do this monthly, but I realize that isn't always feasible. You'll also want to make sure that you keep the door seals clean so that you get a proper seal and that the fans are clear of any debris that may stop them from operating at their full potential. If you have a chest freezer, this applies as well.

The average family has their refrigerator thermostat turned way too high. Ideally, you should set it to 3. This will keep your foods the correct temp and prevent your fridge from having to work hard (a.k.a. use more energy) to maintain that temp. Your fridge also works best when it's *not* completely full as it needs air to circulate. Your freezer on the other hand will work best when it *is* full. If you don't have enough groceries on hand, grab a few bottles of water and use them to fill in gaps. Not only will they help your freezer stay colder so it works less, but in the event of a power outage they'll help keep your food fresh longer! That's a win/win if you ask me!

For your washer and dryer, clean the out rim of the lid and any locking mechanisms monthly. Also, give the tub a good cleaning by running a small empty load with only 1 cup of vinegar added. Make sure that your lint trap is cleaned before every use and if you use fabric softener sheets on a regular basis, run some vinegar over your lint trap. Fabric softener can have a plug effect on the mesh of the trap causing lint to get trapped making it a fire hazard. Once every month or so, you should also be looking at the actual dryer vent and washer hoses to be sure there is nothing stuck in them and that they're in good shape with no cracks or rips.

A CLEAN FURNACE FILTER IS YOUR FRIEND

Furnace filters are what keep your furnace from spewing dust and other nastiness through your heating/cooling vents and they can get extremely nasty. Your filters need to be changed every 3 months at the absolute minimum. Ideally, you should be changing them monthly, but I do realize that that isn't always possible. When your filter is dirty, the a/c compressor and heater must work twice as hard. This means more power usage which in turn, means more money out of your pocket.

QUALITY VS. QUANTITY

I mentioned that I bought my washer, dryer and fridge new and now you might be asking why I bought new instead buying used. I tried to buy used, but was unable to find a deal that I liked on appliances that I trusted. We were on a very tight time crunch, so I had two choices; buy new and get reliability with a warranty or buy used where I wasn't comfortable and possibly deal with broken appliances after a couple of weeks. I chose reliability and knowing that my money went to items that I was sure about.

Quality versus quantity can be an incredibly hard lesson to learn, but it is one that most of us only need to learn once. Simply put, cheap items will usually cost you more in the long run because you usually must replace them more often.

In the case of my appliances, the only "deals" that I could find were ones that I was not sure would run the way I needed them to without significant repair. Sure, I could have bought a washer for around fifty dollars, but I would have likely had to have spent several hundred more for repair (or even a replacement) when it didn't last. I value my money more than that.

Save on Your Utilities

Utility bills are unfortunately, a necessary evil in our lives. What they don't have to be though is a money draining virus on our budgets. When controlled, the costs of your utility bills can become an easy thing that just must be paid every month. Controlling them takes work though and isn't something that can't be done by just one person in the family. It **must** be a whole family exercise or it's a futile exercise.

Working together as a family can get your utility bills to a place where you can easily manage them and easily pay them on time every single month. Keep in mind that you likely won't notice drops within the first month because of billing cycles so be sure you give them a month or two before you give up and you'll start seeing results.

Slash Your Power Bill

We all know that things like turning off lights and opening windows can help, but what about the rest of it? You can significantly drop your bill if you're looking to, but I'm not going to lie to you or fluff things up. Dropping your electric bill more than a few dollars a month requires commitment.

For instance, ours used to run very high at around five hundred a month or more no matter what we did. Then we made one seemingly small change and it dropped to only ninety dollars per month.

THE CURIOUS CASE OF THE POWER EATING MONSTER

Want to know what caused our electric bill to run three hundred dollars or more per month? I did too so I went on a mission (*complete with spy music and Mission Impossible movements just for fun*) and spent three solid months tracking our usage, how often appliances and electronics were used, whether lights were shut off and more. What I found was that we had a power eating monster that was otherwise known as....

Our central air.

We live in Texas. In case you're not familiar? Anyone who lives here can tell you that Texas has 4 seasons, but they're not the ones you learned in school. Instead, we have almost summer, summer, still summer and Christmas. Plainly put? It gets hot here. Melt the sidewalk, fry an egg on the hood, sweat becomes your constant companion hot. To put it mildly, we were extremely discouraged to figure out that our beloved air conditioning was the cause of such an expensive power bill.

For us though, it didn't matter. Five hundred dollars a month is way more than I want to pay for power so we made the decision to turn the a/c off and to use box fans and open windows except for during July and August, the two hottest months of the year. Those two months are simply too hot here to avoid using the a/c.

Because we're only using the a/c when we truly needed to, our electric bill dropped to $89.00 a month. I would rather be financially fit than a cool 69 degrees. Now *that* is a bill that I don't mind paying. We're perfectly cool the rest of the year with fans and open windows and the money we save pays for the two months each year that we run the air conditioning. It's a win/win situation all around!

Keeping Your Home Cool Without A/C

If you're wanting to ditch the a/c for a bit, you'll need to find a new way to keep your home cool. To do this easily, open the windows. At one end of the room(s), place a box fan in the window facing inward. At the other end, place a box fan in the window facing outward.

What this will do is circulate air within the room and help keep it cooler. You won't have an ice-cold room, but it will be much more bearable than if you skipped the fans.

One word of caution: As I said, we run our a/c during July and August. It isn't because we can't stand the heat. It is simply because the temperatures can get so high during those months that it is truly dangerous not to have a cooler home. If you, like me, live in an area where summer temperatures frequently reach three digits, please run the a/c when you should.

No amount of saved money is worth your health or life.

Set it and Forget It

Know that thermostat box that sits near the furnace and central air unit? Set it two degrees warmer than you would like to and then forget that it even exists. You won't be uncomfortable with a two-degree change, but that two degrees is more than enough to make a difference in you power and heating bills.

PROGRAM IT

Does your home have a programmable thermostat or one of the older slide or dial ones? If you answered slide or dial, it may be time to think about upgrading it. Those types of thermostats are very hard to regulate and can cause your furnace or air to run longer and harder than it should.

A programmable thermostat on the other hand, only does what you tell it to do. When you set it for a specific temperature, it won't run until it needs to.

SEALING UP LEAKS

Small air leaks can be detrimental to your electric bill and they can pop up in the most unexpected places. As an example, a few years ago, we lived in a home where the kitchen cabinets let air through due to the type of foundation we had. I would have never guessed that my kitchen cabinets could be causing my home to leak air.

To find those leaks, take a walk around the walls of each room in your home. Be sure to run your hand around all windows, doors, baseboards and where the walls meet the floor. You'll also want to check each closet that your home has. It might surprise you to know that in some homes, especially older ones, closets are not surrounded by the same insulation that the rest of the home has. Plug or seal any leaks that you find to save and keep your home more comfortable.

PHANTOM ELECTRIC

Have you ever heard the term "phantom electric?" I'm guessing not, but you very likely know what it is even if you don't know what it's called. Those appliances and electronics you have in your home use power...even if they're not currently turned on. A good example of this is the little light on your computer monitor that stays lit even after it is powered off. The electric that they use is power you are paying for, but never really "seeing."

That is phantom electric and yes, it's costing you money. In fact, it's likely costing you at least an extra hundred per year in extra electric costs.

To cut this cost, start unplugging things when they aren't in use. That can get tedious though so using a power strip or surge protector can make it easier. You'll have one cord to unplug versus several at a time.

A few common appliances and electronics that use phantom electric:

- Cell phone chargers
- Game Systems
- Tablet chargers
- Televisions
- DVD and Blu-ray players
- Speakers
- Lamps
- Microwave
- Toasters
- Toaster Ovens
- Coffeemakers

THE SINGLE MOST EXPENSIVE APPLIANCE YOU OWN

Can you name the one appliance that is in every home that costs the most to run? This appliance doesn't have to cost as much to run as it does though. Most people will guess that the fridge is the answer, but those people would be wrong.

Your clothes dryer is the single most expensive appliance in your home to operate. It uses approximately 6% more energy than any other appliances. At a top shelf rate of almost fifty cents per load, ask yourself if it's worth it when there is no reason to use one other than convenience.

Instead, line drying can save you thousands over the course of a couple of years and I do mean thousands. If your dryer is costing you one-hundred dollars a month *(and chances are, it is)*, over a two-year period, you will have paid twenty-four hundred dollars just to use it on top of the initial cost to purchase it.

By contrast, a clothes line and clothes pin will run you around ten dollars, dries your clothes just as well and will cost you nothing more than a few minutes of your time.

We have a dryer, but we only use it for very specific things. I personally don't like the texture of line dried towels, so we dry ours in the dryer. Out of 10 loads of laundry, our dryer gets used for around 2 of them so even though we're using it occasionally, we're still saving a vast amount of money by not making it our primary way to dry

THE BONUS OF NOT DRYING EVERYTHING

Using a clothes dryer is extremely hard on your clothing and causes them to wear out much quicker than they should. Line drying your clothes protects your clothing from this wear meaning that they last longer. Because they last longer, you can avoid having to spend the money on replacing them for much longer.

TINY SPACES AND COLD WEATHER

If you live in an apartment or in an area that is plagued by snow and ice during the winter, line drying won't always be feasible for you. What is feasible though is using a drying rack. These racks can be picked up for around $40.00 each and are typically small enough to fit inside of your tub. They give you the option to avoid using the dryer if you would want to.

SMALL ACTIONS ADD UP

Don't stop at cutting your bill with just these tips though. Continue to work at getting it lower and lower until you're sure it can't be dropped anymore. Be careful not to make the mistake of overlooking something just because it's a small task and won't save you a boatload of cash. Those small savings are the ones that save your budget most of the time.

SLASH YOUR WATER BILL

Do you know that I've spoken with people who are perfectly comfortable paying upwards of one hundred fifty dollars per month for water? That seems more than a bit high to me and hopefully it does to you as well. Water is one of those bills that there is only so much you can do to save because we use so much of it on a regular basis. That doesn't mean that there aren't ways to save, just that I personally don't think it's the best place to spend years working on. Put your savings methods into place and focus on a different area where you can save more making sure you check in on your water saving tricks every couple of weeks to be sure they're still flowing *(pun intended)* like they should be.

THE FLOATING BOTTLE

Take the back of your toilet off and add a full bottle of water to the back of the tank. The full bottle will displace the water around it and your toilet won't use as much to flush or fill back up. The toilet still works like it should and you'll save on your water bill. Just a piece of advice; when you first add it, keep a close eye on it. Ours floated around the tank and got stuck in the drain causing it to run constantly defeating the entire purpose. To fix the issue, we added a few small rocks to the bottle to weigh it down and keep it from floating around.

SHUT IT OFF

I know you've heard this one probably more times than you can count, but since way too many people forget about it, I think it bears repeating. When you're brushing your teeth, shaving, doing dishes, or anything else that require running water, turn the water off. When you let that excess water go down the drain, you're basically sending your money down the drain with it. Instead, bank those drops and shut the water off while you're brushing your teeth or shaving and only turn it on when you need to rinse. If you're hand washing dishes, fill one side of the sink up with wash water and one side up with rinse water.

GREY WATER

Feeling like taking the last section one step further? Remove part of the drain pipe from under your sinks and drain them into a bucket. Scoop the bath water from the tub when you're done into a bucket. Use the buckets of "grey water" to flush the toilet, water the plants (don't use water that has ANY soap residue or food particles on your plants), wash the car, and more. In most cases, the water is perfectly fine and you'll be getting one last use out of something that most people consider useless. If you can't think of what to use soapy water for, shut off the water for the back of your toilet tank and pour grey water into the bowl to force flush it.

HAND WASH YOUR CLOTHING

Remember that talk we had earlier about the washer? It not only costs you electric, but it adds a lot to your water bill. If you're wanting to go hardcore saver, grab a bucket and a plunger (use a clean one please) and use the set up to hand wash your clothes. Your clothes will come out cleaner and they'll last longer as well since there will be less wear and tear on them from the machine.

I have certain clothing items that must be hand washed to keep their quality. To avoid having to stand at the sink and scrub clothes, I picked up a portable washer called a

WonderWash. It is a medium sized egg shaped tub that is hand cranked. I use less water with this than I would by hand washing and it is considerably easier to do.

FILL THE TUB

Showers are a huge waste of water and despite the common though, baths are much more economical when it comes to the cost of your water. Newer shower heads use around 2 gallons of water per minute, but older ones can easily dump as much as 4 gallons per minute down the drain. For a 20-minute shower, that's as many as 80 gallons of water going down your drain.

Instead, fill up the tub and take a bath. It may seem like filling your tub uses more water, but it doesn't. If you don't like the idea of bathing in "dirty water," take your bath then hop in the shower for a quick rinse. Just keep it to 60 seconds or less since all that you would be doing is rinsing off any bath water residue.

If you absolutely must take a shower, limit yourself to five minutes for men and seven to eight minutes for women. That's plenty of time to do what you need to do without wasting water and money.

SAVE IN THE GARAGE

Aside from your home, your car is probably the second biggest expense that you have. Gas costs, repair costs, even your car payment can all be some of the biggest budget busters you'll find. All hope isn't lost though. There are quite a few things you can do though to save on not your car, but on the daily operations and the costs of maintaining it.

MAKE WISE DECISIONS BEFORE YOU BUY

Ask just about any money smart millionaire and you'll find that a lot of them drive used cars. The reason behind it is simple. 1. New cars are really, overpriced and 2. The value of your car drops significantly as soon as you drive it off the lot. Instead of buying new? Check out a good used car. Personally, we drive a 2010 Honda Accord. We bought it used and have never regretted it.

Before you buy make sure to take it to your mechanic and make sure that it's mechanically and structurally sound. The last thing you'll want is to buy a car that has something bent on the frame or that will need major repair work to keep it running. Minor repairs like new brake pads or new tires are perfectly fine for your used car to need since they won't cost you too much and they're not something that is going to continue to break over and over once you do put money into it.

Make a Car Payment to Yourself

If your car is going to need replaced soon, get ahead on the cost and avoid taking a car loan by making car payments to yourself now each month. Figure out what your average car payment would be and instead of paying it to a bank, put it into your own savings account.

By the time that you are ready to purchase your "new" car, you will have enough saved to do so without a loan. This also has the advantage of being able to walk out of the dealership with a better price. Most places will offer you a better deal if you're paying cash versus financing your new vehicle.

Make the Most of Errand Day

One of the biggest drains on gasoline costs is running out over and over throughout the week. When we run errands multiple times each week, we typically end up spending more since we're in and out of stores or other businesses more often. Save all your errands for one single day each week and run them all on that day. Your budget and your car will thank you.

As I mentioned earlier, one of the best ways to save on gas cost is to combine your grocery shopping with a store that gives a discount on gas or even gift cards for gas stations. Those fuel points can save you big per gallon on gas. Case in point? We recently cashed in our fuel points and ended up paying less than $1.00 per gallon on gas.

One awesome strategy that I've seen used is the gift card/fuel points combo. If one of your local stores offers a fuel discount per dollar spent, use that to your advantage by picking up gift cards for other stores that you regularly shop at. By doing so you will build up fuel points on money that you were planning on spending anyhow.

Did I not explain that well? **Here's one example of how it could work:**

Grocery store A offers fuel points for every dollar that I spend.

Week 1 you need to shop $50.00 each at Amazon.com, Walmart and plan on ordering pizza from Pizza Hut. You head to grocery store A to purchase a $50 Amazon gift card, a $50 Walmart gift card and a $25 Pizza Hut gift card.

You were spending that $125 anyhow so you're not out any extra money by purchasing gift cards. The difference is that now you have $125 extra for your fuel points than you would have if you had spent the money without the gift cards.

MAINTAIN THINGS PROPERLY

Proper car maintenance is an absolutely, can't put it off, must happen, must do for keeping your auto costs down. A vehicle that isn't maintained can easily turn into both a money pit and a headache without any warning. To keep this from happening, make sure that your car is being tuned up on time.

Oil changes, spark plugs, battery maintenance, alignments and regular tire maintenance are all important to have done. Your oil should be changed, at a very minimum, every 5,000 miles. Your spark plugs, battery and alignment should be checked once every 6 months to ensure that they're all working or functioning the way that they should. Your tires should be checked once every few months as well to be sure they're properly inflated.

AIR UP & INSPECT ON A REGULAR BASIS

Be 100% certain that your tires are properly inflated. Underinflated tires can cause you to spend around 3% more in gas costs, *and* are at a higher risk for blowing out. Blowouts can cause you big bucks depending on the amount of damage done. We had a blowout a while back due to a tire that we didn't realize had been damaged. The tire blew out while we were doing 70/mph down the interstate. It ended up costing us more than five hundred dollars in body work to our front fender just to fix the damage done to it on top of the cost of a new tire.

Make sure that you're also inspecting things like your wipers, doors and any other moving parts on your car regularly too. Staying ahead of anything breaking is one surefire way to make sure that you don't end up wasting money.

CH-CH-CH-CHANGES

Want to hear a "funny" story? Okay, you might find it funny, but I certainly didn't then and still sort of don't. I once blew up a Toyota Camry while driving down the interstate. How? It threw a rod and bam! Instant smoke, fire and finding myself sitting stuck on the side of the road in the middle of winter.

How did I pull off such an awesome feat you ask? By not bothering to change the oil...at all...in the entire time I owned it. As a matter of fact, I don't recall doing much maintenance on it at all. Granted, I was young when it happened, but those mistakes cost me drastically. Had I done a twenty-dollar oil change, my car likely would have been on the road for a lot longer. Don't make the same mistake that I did.

Save on Entertainment

Entertainment is one area that can easily be overshot on our budget. In truth, it can be hard to estimate how much you'll be spending, especially if you're heading some place like an amusement park or carnival. I've found the best way to stay in budget, but still visit those fun sites is to overshoot the amount of money we think we will need. If I think that we'll be paying one-hundred dollars for something, I will budget one-hundred fifty dollars just in case I'm wrong or we run into an extra expense.

Finding Frugal (or FREE!) Fun

Sometimes the most fun you can have is something that doesn't cost a ton or is even free. There seems to be a common misconception in society today that to have fun, we must spend a lot. It simply isn't true and in fact, there's plenty of fun that is budget friendly if you just get a bit creative.

Put the Library to Good Use

These days everyone has a Kindle or an e-reader of some sort and because of that, they tend to forget that the library exists. I can tell you that it does and guess what? It's free to use! Head over and grab a few books, a couple of movies and save your cash!

For kids, most libraries have story time, plays and more to keep them entertained! There is nothing better in my mind than my daughter having fun while learning at the same time!

Oh, wait, yes there is...my daughter having fun while learning for free!

VISIT A BOOKSTORE

Along the lines of the library, bookstores are awesome free fun! Most have coffee shops in them (or take your own coffee) so you can sip and shop. Relax on a cozy couch and check out a new book by someone you've never heard of. Also, be sure to check their events calendars for author signings, free readings, or other free events that may be taking place soon for more free fun.

TAKE IN A DOLLAR MOVIE

Most cities have a dollar theater in them and they are a great way to see a flick on the big screen for less. See a movie at your local dollar theater for as little as $1 and because you saved so much on the price of a ticket, you may be able to splurge on a large popcorn or get a dessert after.

FIND A FREE CONCERT

Many local high schools or community colleges offer free concerts that are open to the public. This is a great way to see a live show for less. This is a great way to try some new music varieties and observe some of the local talent.

PUPPY LOVE

Head to your local animal shelter and volunteer for a few hours. You can play with the puppies, help groom them, and have a blast being around the animals. This is a great way to spend time together while also helping a good cause, but most of all...puppies!

MUSEUM DAY

Grab the family and head out to visit a museum. A lot of museums will have free or discounted admission days. Use these days to learn about something new with your better half. You'll be expanding your minds while not expanding your wallet. If you know you're going to be visiting museums often, check into a membership to save even more. In fact, you can grab a membership to the Association of Science-Technology Center Passport program for around twenty-five dollars. This one museum membership allows your family to visit more than 275 science and technology museums across the nation and more than 30 worldwide. Sounds like a pretty good deal for twenty-five dollars!

RIDE BIKES

They say once you learn how to ride a bike that you never forget so even if it's been years, grabbing a bike and heading out for a ride by yourself or with the family is a fantastic way to have some fun. You'll also have the added benefit of getting (or keeping yourself) healthy which saves you money too!

If you must buy bikes, you can still do it on the cheap by checking out thrift stores for them. My daughter's bike was bought from the Goodwill for $12.00. It was brand new, still had the price tags on it and only needed some air put in the tires that cost me .75¢ to use a gas station air machine. Because my husband and I already had bikes, we can now do family bike outings for a final cost of $12.75.

Save on beauty & HBA

It has become far too common in today's world for us to just drop money on the latest beauty treatment or product, but if we were honest with ourselves, we'd admit that 98% of what is currently in our bathroom isn't needed.

Yes, we all need shampoo and soap to keep ourselves clean, but did you realize that you can make those items yourself and save a ton over the course of a year? We stopped buying commercially made beauty products a long time ago for more than one reason. We did it to save money, to use less chemicals in our home and for a few other reasons. As we've gone through the process of replacing those commercial items with homemade ones though, we've found that we prefer the items that I make here at home.

To start, you may want to just replace one item at a time. We did it that way to not only give ourselves time to get used to the homemade items, but also time to find recipes that we liked. If you've tried homemade products before and haven't liked them, give them a second chance with a new recipe since not every person will adore every single recipe that they come across.

We make everything from our own shampoo to shave cream and even beauty scrubs. Doing so has saved us well over $1500 this year alone and our entire family feels better as a whole.

We took homemade beauty a step farther though and now, we make a lot of our own health items too. Things like vapor rub, foot cream and more can all be made at home too. What we found was that my homemade products? Work so much better than the ones we can buy at the store so we don't have a need to buy them anymore.

A WORD ABOUT COST

When you first start making your own beauty and health items, you might be surprised at the out of pocket cost and think that you'll be spending more. It's very true that a lot of the ingredients to make the recipes can add up, but you will need to look at the long run.

A pound of beeswax for ointments might cost you $10.00, but you will get so many uses out of that pound that each batch of whatever you're making ends up costing less than $0.10 worth of beeswax. Coconut oil might run you $15.00 for a tub, but you will get so many uses, that each batch might only use $0.25 worth of that $15.00.

Yes, you will spend more out of pocket at first, but in the long run, you will save so much more.

ESSENTIAL OILS

You'll notice that almost all the recipes below use essential oils and there is a reason for that. Essential oils have been around and used for thousands of years in medicine, cleaning and beauty. Knowing that little tidbit, it only makes sense to include them in your homemade beauty products.

A quick word about EO's and yes, I'm about to make some people very mad with this statement.

There is no such thing as a therapeutic grade oil.

I know…how can I say such a thing, right? Because there simply isn't. *There is no grading system for essential oils in place to create that therapeutic grade that so many different essential oil companies claim. In fact, any essential oil company can label itself as therapeutic grade with no oversight or proof of such a claim.*

What there is though is pure oil versus oil that has been cut with something. Pure oil is just that. It is the essential oil you are looking for in its purest form. There are no addictions, carrier oils or anything else in that bottle of oil. Oil that has been cut usually has a carrier oil or something else mixed into the bottle.

To be safe with your oils, don't bother with that therapeutic grade claim. Instead, look for oils that are 100% pure only. Also, remember that if you're pregnant, you need to check with your doctor before using any essential oil. Some are not safe for use during pregnancy due to their effect.

Base Healing Ointment Recipe

If you're looking at making your own ointments for whatever reasons, there's no need to have several different recipes. Instead, use a base ointment recipe and tweak it to what you want to use it for with the correct essential oils for your purpose.

This recipe is my base recipe. If I want a creamier texture, I use a bit less beeswax. If I'm looking for an ointment texture, I use a bit more. Other than that, I never change it much.

You will need:

- ¼ cup coconut oil
- 2 Tbsp. beeswax pellets
- 1 T. shea butter

This recipe fills a 4oz mason jar. To create your ointment, add the 3 ingredients to your jar then melt in 30 second intervals in the microwave. Stir after each 30 seconds. Once it's melted, add the essential oils you are using and stir well. Put a lid on it and store in a cool, dry place.

HOMEMADE LAVENDER DIAPER RASH CREAM

I don't have any in diapers anymore, but I wish I had known this recipe when I did. Lavender is known for calming rashes, cuts, bruises and crying babies. Because of that, this cream works very well for not only diaper rash, but bug bites, burns and more.

You Will Need:

- Base Healing Ointment Recipe
- 12-15 drops lavender essential oil

Melt the base ointment recipe in a 4oz mason jar. Once melted, add the essential oil and stir well. Let cool completely before using. Use like commercial diaper rash cream.

Homemade Vapor Rub

My husband and daughter both suffer from severe seasonal allergies. To combat them, we use locally grown honey (to help build a resistance) and this vapor rub recipe if they still get congested.

You Will Need:

- Base Healing Ointment Recipe (You may want to add a bit more beeswax to get a true ointment for this one).
- 5-15 drops Peppermint Essential Oil (depending on how strong you want the scent)
- 5-15 drops Eucalyptus Essential Oil (depending on strength)

Melt the base healing ointment recipe is a 4oz mason jar. Once melted, add the essential oils and mix well. Store in a cool, dry place. Apply to chest, bottom of feet and upper lip to help relieve congestion. If the scent isn't strong enough to work like a vapor rub, add more essential oil. Be VERY careful though not to add too much.

HOMEMADE HEADACHE SALVE

I have suffered from migraines since I was a teenager. This salve recipe came into creation because I had one at the beginning of this year that just would not let go. Since then, I've made this my go to with headaches and it works like a charm.

You Will Need:

- Base Healing Ointment Plus 1-2 tablespoons extra beeswax
- 12-15 Lavender Essential Oil
- 8-10 Peppermint Essential Oil

Melt base healing ointment recipe in a 4oz mason jar. Once melted, add the essential oils and mix well. To use, apply to temples and lie down in a cool, dark room.

HOMEMADE SLEEP SALVE

This one came about because both my daughter and I have trouble getting to sleep. Lavender is well known for helping calm and inducing sleep. We use it every night in our home and we've never slept better.

You Will Need:

- Base Healing Ointment Recipe Plus 1-2 tablespoons extra beeswax
- 15-20 drops Lavender essential oil

Melt base healing ointment then mix in essential oils. Store in a cool, dry place. To use, rub on tubby at bedtime.

Homemade Healing Lotion for Dry Skin

This lotion recipe has quickly become my favorite lotion recipes period. I have extremely dry skin and literally nothing that I have ever bought worked. My recipe though? Clears up the dry skin issue with one or two applications and keeps it away too. As a side benefit, this recipe also works very well as a wrinkle reducer since it contains Vitamin E oil.

You will need:

- 1 cup coconut oil
- ¼- ½ tsp Vitamin E Oil
- 10 drops Lavender essential oil
- 8 drops Peppermint essential oil

Melt the coconut oil in a double boiler or over low heat. Once it's about half way melted, add the vitamin E oil and stir to combine until the oil is fully melted and clear. Once the oil is melted, pour it into a metal mixing bowl and stash the bowl, your mixer beaters and all in the freezer for fifteen to twenty minutes.

Pull the bowl out of the freezer and beat on high for 3 minutes. At this point your coconut oil will be a cloudy color. Scrape the sides of the bowl down then add the essential oils. Continue mixing until it is well combined and fully whipped! Store it in an airtight jar in a cool place. If you leave it in a super warm or humid room, it can turn back to oil but you should be able to whip it up again without too many issues. Just make sure you chill it again if you need to. Coconut oil has a melting point around 76 degrees so keep that in mind. If you want to avoid it melting down, store it in the fridge but make sure you label it very well so no one thinks it's food.

GREEN TEA & PEPPERMINT BATH SOAK

I have chronic pain issues as well as chronic fatigue issues. This was one of the reasons we moved to a more natural home. We discovered that chemical and commercial products aggravated my pain levels so we needed to remove them. This bath soak has been a lifesaver for me. It helps soothe the pain and swelling that I have and energizes me as well. Plus? It's super easy to make which is always a plus in my book.

You Will Need:

- 3 cups Epsom Salt
- 1 cup finely ground Sea Salt
- 3 tablespoons loose green tea or 9 tea bags
- 4-6 drops Peppermint Essential Oil
- 6-8 drops fractionated coconut or almond oil

Combine the 3 cups of Epsom salt and the 1 cup of sea salt in a medium mixing bowl and stir well to make sure they're fully mixed. If you're using green tea bags, cut them open to remove the tea. Add the tea to the salt mixture and stir again to make sure they're mixed very well. You want to be sure that you have a even distribution of the tea.

Add the peppermint oil and either the coconut or almond oil and stir it well to combine. If your skin is dry, use the coconut oil. If your skin is oily, go with the almond oil. You can use a bit more than called for if it doesn't go far enough, but you shouldn't have to when you're adding the essential oil to it as well. Stir very well to make sure the oils get distributed. When mixed well, cover with a paper or kitchen towel and let sit for an hour or so to absorb the scent and oil. Store in an airtight container in a dry place.

To use, scoop ½ cup to 1 cup into a warm bath, grab a good book and enjoy your soak!

HOMEMADE AFTERSHAVE

My hubby is beardly so we don't have to make this one very often, but when I do, he adores it. He says it cools and soothes so much better than anything he's ever bought from the store.

You will need:

- 1/4 cup Aloe Vera
- 1/4 cup witch hazel
- 1 tablespoon carrier oil of your choice
- 5 Drops Juniper essential oil
- 2 Drops Peppermint Essential oil

To make, fill the bottle you are using with the aloe, carrier oil and essential oils. Top the bottle off with the witch hazel and shake well. Make sure you give it a good shake before using and use just like you would with any commercial aftershave.

Mint Chocolate Chip Body Butter

I love anything mint scented or flavored so when I was looking at making my own body butter, I immediately went to mint. What I like about this one is that it cools and soothes as well as moisturizing so when my legs are having chronic pain issues, it is a small help.

You Will Need:

- 1/2 cup Cocoa Butter
- 1/2 cup Coconut Oil
- 10 – 25 drops peppermint essential oil (depending on how strong you like it)

To start, scrape your cocoa butter out. Be sure you don't melt it for this recipe. You want it solid so just use a butter knife to chunk it off or scrape it out of the container if needed. Next, add the cocoa butter and coconut oil to a medium mixing bowl. Add the peppermint oil then mix with your mixer. A stand mixer works best for this, but you absolutely can use a hand mixer if you need. It will just take a bit longer to whip. Continue whipping in 1-2 minute intervals making sure you stop in between to scrape the sides of the bowl down. If you're using a stand mixer, it should only take 8-10 minutes to whip, but a hand mixer might take a few minutes longer.

Scoop into an airtight container and store in a cool, dry place. If you want a firmer texture, melt 1-2 tablespoons of beeswax pellets and whip it into your homemade body butter. Start small and add more as needed since beeswax hardens so quickly.

Homemade Coconut Shampoo

When we realized just how much of our budget was going to shampoo *(1 woman with long hair + 1 tween girl with long hair = you do the math)*, I knew I had to find a way to cut that cost. Sure, I could use coupons, but since we were already trying to go all natural, I wanted something I could make at home. This recipe is the result of that.

You Will Need:

- ½ cup coconut milk
- ⅔ cup unscented Castile soap
- 2 tsp. vegetable glycerin
- 1 tsp. Jojoba oil
- 15-20 drops essential oil of your choice

In a quart-sized mason jar, combine all the ingredients except your essential oils and stir gently to combine. If you have an empty shampoo bottle or two, you can mix it up in them instead to make it easier to use if you want. Add 15-20 drops of your favorite essential oil (or use one of the combinations below) and stir gently again to mix the oils well into the mixture. Seal with a lid and ring and store in a cool place. Yes, the fridge is fine.

To use, apply a generous amount to your hair beginning at the ends and work your way up to the roots. Let it sit for 1-2 minutes then rinse away completely. For an added shine and extra conditioning boost, rinse with apple cider vinegar after shampooing.

Have a specific hair issue you need to solve? Use these essential oil combos in your shampoo when you mix it up:

Dry Hair:

- Lavender
- Rosemary
- Geranium

Oily Hair:

- Rosemary
- Peppermint
- Cypress
- Basil

Dry Scalp:

- Rosemary
- Clary Sage
- Tea Tree
- Lemon
- Lavender

To Add Shine:

- Rosemary
- Chamomile

HOMEMADE SHAVE CREAM

This one works well for both men and women. You can target for each by what essential oil you use. Lavender and Rosemary are great for women, while Idaho Blue Spruce is a great option for men.

You Will Need:

- ⅓ cup coconut oil
- ⅓ cup Shea butter
- 1 Tbsp. unscented Castille soap
- 10-15 drops Essential oil of your choice

In a large mixing bowl or the mixing bowl of your stand mixer, combine the Shea butter and coconut oil until well combined. If you don't have a stand mixer, no worries. You can use a hand mixer with the same results.

Mix until it has fluffed up to nearly triple its original amount. This usually takes 3-5 minutes, but your times may vary.

Add the Castille soap and essential oil and whip again for 1-2 minutes or until it is well combined.

That's it! Totally done in under 10 minutes! Store your shave cream in a jar with a lid. If you want a thicker consistency, store it in the fridge, clearly labeled. In bathrooms or bedrooms that are warm, it may liquefy a bit. It's okay if that happens, just whip it back up before using. To use, wet the skin down and apply generously. Shave then rinse well.

Relationships & Money

Did you know that the leading cause for divorce in the United States is financial issues? Just in case that didn't get the point across, I'll say it again. If you're fighting about money, your relationship is going to have a hard go at it. It doesn't matter whether you're married or just living together, if your finances are together (and if you're married or living together, they should be), they can and will directly impact your relationship.

Joint Bank Accounts

The first step to a healthy financial relationship with your partner is a joint bank account. I know, some of you are now feeling like they want to throw this book into the wall and call me an old-fashioned fool who just set back women's lib a hundred years.

Hear me out though: In a situation where one person's sole income goes into a sole checking account, it prevents two things. One person in the relationship cannot access the money at all. In an emergency, they can't get funds to help. What if your spouse is on a business trip and you need cash for a flat tire? With a sole account, you can't get the money to fix that tire until you get in contact with your spouse and have them send it to you which could end up costing you not only time, but money lost if you miss your business meeting.

The other reason for a joint bank account is that this prevents one spouse from overspending behind the other's back. If you are both involved in the banking, there are no surprise splurges, no habits and no issues that the other doesn't know about. This will prevent your family from going broke but having no idea as to why it happened and it will build trust between you and your partner making for a much happier relationship. Remember that story I told earlier in the book? The wife had no idea that the husband was spending all their money on a gambling addiction. In addition to tracking their expenses, a joint account where she could easily see what was happening could have helped to prevent this.

START PLANNING FOR RETIREMENT NOW

If you don't already have one, start an IRA with your local bank or 401k plan at your jobs. Planning now for retirement 30 years down the road will ensure that you can retire with the life that you want. While there are four types of IRA's, only 2 of them will apply to the majority. All of them have different eligibility rules and different tax rules so you may not qualify to have one or another.

With a traditional IRA, you can often save on your taxes by deferring them until you retire which is when your IRA would become subject to income tax. The contributions to a traditional IRA are also tax deductible for a lot of folks which can make it even more attractive to some. Usually, you will want to go with a traditional IRA if you are worried that you might be in a lower tax bracket (i.e. lower income) during retirement **and** you won't need the money until you're at least age 59 ½ since there can be penalties for withdrawing it early.

Another option, the Roth IRA, is basically an individual savings account, however, it does have certain eligibility rules that you'll want to consider. What makes a Roth IRA attractive to some is the fact that even though your contributions are not tax-free, qualified withdraws are. A Roth IRA tends to be better if you think you'll be in a higher tax bracket after retirement, want to leave money to your heirs, and might want to withdraw funds before you retire.

Before you make your decision, make sure you speak with a qualified financial advisor. They will be able to advise you which one is best for you and which will give you the best growth.

I know that if you're young, retirement is likely one of the last things you are thinking about. Unfortunately, that is the exact reason that so many people are unable to retire. Learning how to plan your retirement now and putting that plan into action is the only way to ensure that you'll be able to stop working when you and your spouse or partner are ready. Planning as a couple can help improve your relationship.

LIVE WITHIN YOUR MEANS

I know that we're far into this book and I'm just now mentioning it, but living within your means is so important to a healthy relationship and a healthy financial status. Living above your means will only cause stress, problems and may just cause your life together to end differently than you planned. Living within your means, however large or small that is, ensures that you will always have everything that you need as a couple and that you don't accrue debt, monthly expenses or other issues that your budget can't handle.

You'll both need to be on the same page when it comes to spending. If one of you is a spender and one is thrifty, it will only serve to cause strife in the marriage or relationship. It's easy to cut that off at the pass though by planning your budget together and keeping each other on track.

A weekly budget meeting is how my husband and I keep things straight. We sit down together and go over our spending for the week, our bills and our investments together to make sure that we're on track with where we want to be.

LINES OF COMMUNICATION

This may seem like a no-brainer but for some, it's not. We live in a society that is so dominated by smart phones and tablets that it can be easy to remember to just talk to each other. Talk about your finances together. Talk about your dreams together. Talk about your fears. If you aren't talking, you're not working together and this...of all things...could be the downfall of your marriage. By talking to each other about the things that matter, you're letting one another in and you're setting up a relationship that will last a lifetime.

FRUGAL DATING

Whether you're married or just in a long-term relationship, date night is one of those things that is a must for keeping a relationship alive. Couples must have that alone time to talk and continue to get to know each other. You might think that you know your husband or wife, but trust me, you don't.

People change from day to day; their thoughts and opinions change, their wants and desires change. Having a weekly or monthly date night allows you to stay caught up on each other. Plus? Who doesn't need a little bit more romance in their lives?

DATE NIGHT IN -

Dates don't have to be away from home. In fact, some of the most memorable ones my husband and I have had have been without leaving the house. Gather a few blankets, spread them out on the floor, pop some popcorn and cuddle in the dark while you watch sappy romance movies (or whatever genre the two of you like) together. My husband and I enjoy finding cheesy "b" class movies on Netflix, turning down the sounds and making up our own words to the outrageously bad acting. Watch whatever the two of you happen to be in the mood for. You out of pocket cost? Only the popcorn!

STARGAZING

Get out of the house, find a lake or pond, go lie on the banks and watch the stars together. Of course, this only works if the weather cooperates, but if it does, you're in like Flynn! Grab a comfy blanket, pack some romantic snacks (strawberries, sparkling cider, etc) and some sparkling cider. Watch the stars over the lake while you talk and get to know each other again! You could even hold a contest to see how many constellations you can each name with the winner taking a small prize. Anything you can come up with works, but a small amount of healthy competition is good for any relationship.

GO ROLLER SKATING

I can't be the only one who has fond memories of the skating rink growing up, can I? If you do too, grab your honey and find a skating rink nearby. Usually you can pay admission and rent skates for under ten dollars per person and you'll both have fun seeing who can still stand and skate on them or which one of you falls flat on your rear. If you do this though, please remember that there are likely going to be kids around as well so it's probably a good idea to keep your PDA's to a minimum on this date.

Not So Fancy Dinner

One of the cutest dates that I ever had planned for me was a dinner that involved a popular, affordable fast food restaurant. Send the kids to the sitter and set the table for a candlelit dinner. Use the fancy china, use the nice candlesticks and turn the lights down low. Turn on some romantic music to set the atmosphere and serve dinner.

Serve McDonalds.

This type of date is best if your partner has a sense of humor, but it's fun, whimsical and yes, even a bit romantic. It's the type of date that is remembered fondly for years.

KIDS AND MONEY

Teaching your young ones to be thrifty spenders and wise savers is one of the most important lessons you will teach as they grow. You don't have to go into deep detail when they're young, but by the time they leave your home they should know how to manage their own money. Don't rely on the schools to teach money management skills to your kids. I am thirty-two years old and wasn't taught money management in school. If it wasn't common then, it certainly isn't going to be now.

MONEY BASICS

When your kids are younger, start teaching them the basics of not only handling their own money, but earning their own as well. Kids as young four or five can do simple chores to earn a few cents a week. When they're that little something like a quarter for every year of their age is appropriate. As they get older, their allowance and chore "payments" should change to fit their age.

After they reach ten or twelve years old, start teaching them the basics of budgeting. Let them budget their allowance, but keep an eye on them to be sure they're saving instead of spending every dime they have. Make sure that they have a kids savings account too so that they can "see" their savings growing. Most banks offer a youth account that has parental oversight so there isn't any chance of them spending any money without you knowing it. Giving them a strong foundation will only help them as they grow.

CHORES & EARNING THEIR OWN

I don't believe in paying kids just to pay them and I don't believe in paying kids for every single chore they do. In our home, our daughter earns an allowance up to ten dollars per week. To get her allowance, she must earn it by doing chores, however those chores are extra ones on top of her regular ones. For example, if she mows the lawn one week, she earns five dollars of her ten-dollar allowance, but taking out the trash doesn't earn her anything since it's a daily chore that she is expected to do. She is a part of this family and this household and as such, she is required to help with tasks that are a normal part of daily life without expecting payment in return.

ADVANCED MONEY TECHNIQUES

As your kids enter their teenage years, they will need to have a firm grasp on budgeting, balancing a checking account and managing their money fully. Do not let your kids leave home without teaching them these skills. Too many kids today head off to college or the workforce and get into trouble because they lack any money management skills.

LETTING THEM HAVE A LITTLE ROOM

Some banks offer teen checking accounts. These accounts are just like yours, but have a few more restrictions on them. Around age sixteen (or whenever they get their first "real" job), take them and help them sign up for one of these accounts. It will be their first taste at being an adult and one they desperately will need.

THREE BASIC SKILLS YOUR KIDS NEED TO KNOW

Your kids may still be little (or not even born yet), but that doesn't change these skills. I don't mean to imply that these are the only three skills your kids will need to know before they leave home, but if you manage to teach them nothing else, make sure it is these three.

The correlation between working and having money:

Kids don't automatically recognize that they need to work for the things that they get in life, but by the time they're grown they need to. Chores can help with this as can letting them get a job as soon as they're old enough. It doesn't matter how you teach them, but make sure that you do. Otherwise, they'll become an adult and not understand that to make it in life they must work to get there.

How to save money:

Another skill that your kids will absolutely need to know how to do is to save money and it may just surprise you that a very large number of people don't know how to save money and as such never figure it out. By making sure that your kids know how to save, you'll be setting them up to build a solid financial life for themselves where they don't have to scrape and struggle every day.

How to Balance a Checkbook:

You would be surprised at the number of adults who can't balance their checkbook. Even if you don't expect your kids to write checks, they still need to know how to do it so that they can balance their bank account with their debit card transactions to keep their accounts where they should be and balanced. When I was in school, this was taught in basic math classes but I'm told that now it isn't. My daughter is homeschooled so I can't comment as to whether it is or isn't, but even if it is? You still need to reinforce the idea at home.

ONE THING I DO NOT RECOMMEND FOR TEACHING KIDS ABOUT MONEY

The idea of paying kids for doing all chores seems to be a common one these days. Please don't make that mistake with your kids. Yes, my daughter gets paid to do chores, but they are the ones that are above and beyond what her normal ones are. She is a part of this family, she lives in our home with us, she can help keep it clean and orderly just like the rest of us do. Because of this, I refuse to pay her for things like helping with dishes, vacuuming and other daily chores.

The chores that she does get paid for are the ones that are out of the norm such as mowing the grass, washing the car or organizing my food stockpile. Those are the chores that are not her responsibility so if she does them, she deserves to be paid for them. They are also voluntary chores for her. If she doesn't want to do them, she does not have to since again, they're beyond what her normal chores are.

Your kids are the same way. Regular chores should be a part of their daily activities, but the out of the norm ones should be paid for. By doing things this way, you will continue to reinforce the idea that they need to work for the things they want in life.

TEACHING KIDS ABOUT SAVING AND GIVING

As your kids start to earn their own money, you'll need to teach them how to both save and how to give to others. First, sit down with them and help them choose a charity or cause that they believe in. Do yourself and them a favor and let your kids decide where their money is going to go. If you push your favorite charity on them, it will make it harder for them to give. If, however, it's a cause that they believe in, no matter what it is, they'll likely give freely. If they're very little, put it into very simple words such as "you're helping Santa build presents for other little kids" to explain giving to Toys for Tots or some other kids based cause.

When your kids earn their own money, they need to be marking a portion of it as giving, a portion for saving and a portion for spending. Some recommend a 10/10/80 split, others a 20/20/60 split but in the end, it is totally up to you which one your kids follow. Just make sure that they are marking at least some for giving and spending so that they will learn.

FUN (AND FREE!) KIDS ACTIVITIES

Is summer boredom starting to set in? Are the kids spending way too much time in front of the television and their video games? It sounds like it is time for an intervention! Kids activities can be very expensive if you allow them to be, but they don't have to be. In fact, your kids will have just as much, if not more fun at a cheaper event as they would at one that you are struggling to pay for.

LET'S GO FISHING

Head to the local lake or even pond with your fishing poles in tow and see what you can catch! If you don't have poles you can find them at Walmart for as low as twenty dollars. Dig up some fresh worms for free and then see who can catch the most fish. Fishing licenses are typically cheap and most states even have a few specific days or weekends each year where they don't require a license.

HAVE A WATER WAR

Divide the family into teams. Load up with water balloons, the hose, water buckets and go to war! This is a fun way to stay cool while getting wild! The winning team is the one who...well...I'm not sure! You're sure to have fun though!

GET YOUR BAKE ON...KIND OF

When you were a kid what was your favorite part about Mom baking a cake or brownies? Licking the bowl of course! Take a step back from your normal healthy eating and make up a cake mix. Grab a few blankets, pop in a movie and share the cake batter with your child. You will very suddenly become a hero in their eyes because to a kid, unhealthy foods mean greatness.

TRY SOME NATURE CRAFTS

Take crayons and paper and try some leaf rubbings or build your own birdfeeder by rolling a toilet paper tube in peanut butter and then bird seed. Make a bug house out of a jar or you can even make a birdhouse using some scrap wood. Crush berries to make your own paint. Use the bounty of nature and see what else you can create!

GO WILDLIFE WATCHING

Animals are all around us and a very large percentage of kids love them! Grab their backpack and pack up binoculars and spend the day watching the birds, chasing and catching bugs, or seeing what other types of wildlife you can spot while on a nature walk. Look for animal foot prints, feathers, and other evidence of wildlife too. Grab a cheap disposable camera from the dollar store and you can even photograph what you see!

FIND FREE EVENING ENTERTAINMENT.

Find free evening entertainment in your city. Look for outdoor movie screenings. Local colleges and bands tend to offer free concerts in the summer too. Pack a blanket and pack a picnic and head out for a night of food and music. Stay until its dark and you can do a little star gazing after.

One last suggestion:

Two words. Blanket fort.

SAVE ON GIFTS

How much did you spend on the last gift you gave? My guess is that it was expensive. Gifting is very personal and it's something that we all hang hopes on. No one wants to give a bad gift so we buy with the other person in mind hoping that they're going to love it. What we then do is go out and spend more money than we should on gifts; sometimes to the point of hurting our own budget instead of looking at birthdays or any of the other gifting holidays to show just how frugal (but not cheap) you are.

One of the things you'll notice about people who save big on Christmas is that they start shopping very early. In fact, I'm known for starting Christmas and birthday shopping on December 26. Why? Because when you find a deal on something you would like to give as a gift, who cares if it's the holiday season? Buy it cheap and put it up until you need it.

Doing this is a great way to build a gift closet that you can use throughout the year not only for Christmas but for birthdays, anniversaries, house warming gifts and more. Basically, you use extra money that you have in your budget to buy those awesome deals that you find all year. Stash them away in a closet and you'll always have a gift when you need one.

GIFT GIVING TIPS

CLEARANCE IS YOUR FRIEND

Clearance sales should become your new best friend as they can be a huge help in finding affordable gifts. You can find great deals all year long (buy early and stash for when you need them), but the clearance markdowns after Christmas are typically the best. Yes, I start shopping for Christmas and birthdays the day after Christmas.

BLACK FRIDAY & CYBER MONDAY

The day after Thanksgiving and the Monday following it are also two fantastic times of the year to pick up gifts. These sales offer some of the biggest savings you will find all year. Period. If you don't want to brave the stores on Black Friday, you can save just as much by staying at home and shopping online. I shop these sales every year and never leave my office.

GIFT CARD SHOPPING

There are multiple places online that will allow you to earn cashback for shopping or to earn gift cards to places like Amazon, Walmart and some of the bigger stores. You can maximize your gift buying by using one of these places to arm yourself with an arsenal of gift cards to use instead of cash.

As I mentioned earlier, Raise is one of my favorite ways to save on gift cards. Buy them at a discount and get a full priced gift card. Ebay is also a great place to find gift cards for a discount too.

I've included a list of my favorites at the end of this book for you to check out. You never know when you'll find a new tool to help you save.

WHEN ALL ELSE FAILS

A few years ago, giving a homemade gift might have been considered tacky, but these days homemade anything is "all the rage." They're also a very, very budget friendly gift. Things like homemade beauty supplies, kid's crafts, home baked goods or mixes, homemade household goods and more are all sought out making them the perfect gift. If you absolutely can't find a gift to fit your budget, a homemade option just might be the answer.

The recipes for homemade beauty items that I have included above also make fantastic gifts. Package them together in a gift basket and tie a pretty bow on it. You'll be gifting an awesome gift for just a few dollars for each basket.

In addition to those recipes, here are a few more and a few DIY projects that all make great gift ideas. These are all posted on the Six Dollar Family blog and to save us both time and space, I'm simply going to add the links to this chapter. Just copy them exactly into your phone or computer browser or type the links into your browser to view the tutorials.

DIY Snowman Earrings - http://sixdollarfamily.com/diy-snowman-earrings

DIY Wine Cork Keychains - http://sixdollarfamily.com/diy-wine-cork-keychains

Reindeer Noses DIY Gift Idea - http://sixdollarfamily.com/reindeer-noses-diy-gift-idea

Christmas Tree Lightbulb Ornament – http://sixdollarfamily.com/diy-christmas-tree-light-bulb-ornament

Homemade Lavender Lip Scrub - http://sixdollarfamily.com/diy-lavender-lip-scrub

Homemade Raspberry Sugar Scrub – http://sixdollarfamily.com/homemade-raspberry-sugar-scrub

Homemade Orange Sugar Scrub – http://sixdollarfamily.com/diy-orange-sugar-scrub

Oatmeal & Lavender Bath Bombs - http://sixdollarfamily.com/oatmeal-and-lavender-bath-bombs

Homemade Sugar Scrub Bars - http://sixdollarfamily.com/diy-sugar-scrub-bars

Merry Kiss-mas Simple Teacher Gift Idea - http://sixdollarfamily.com/merry-kissmas-simple-teacher-gift-idea

SAVE ON VACATIONS

When the summer months' start rolling in a lot of us start rolling out. Vacations, even short ones, can break our budget quicker than we can blink and before we know it...we're broke. That's the great thing about being frugal though. Wise savers know that there are plenty of easy ways that you can save money on those long (or short) road trips and vacations!

DRIVE VS. FLY

When you first start planning your vacation, the second decision you should make (aside from where to visit) is how you will get there. For some, flying will be much cheaper but for others, driving and a road trip will be the way to go. Make sure you factor in things like plane tickets, baggage fees, taxi's and rental cars if you fly. If you're driving, you'll need to consider gas costs, preventative maintenance on the car, food, drinks and other road trip costs.

SAVE ON AIRFARE

90% of the time, our family drives. It's much cheaper for us to do that than to buy 3 round-trip plane tickets, a rental car and more. However, when I do fly, I pretty much only fly Southwest Airlines. Not only are their fares usually much cheaper than others, but they also allow 2 checked bags and

2 carry-on bags per person. This means that we usually fly without paying any extra baggage fees.

Another trick that I use when I fly is that I almost always fly out early and I do mean crack of dawn early. I've flown as early as 3 a.m. but never later than 7 a.m. Why? Because those flight times are generally much cheaper than flying later in the day. The last time I flew was to Baltimore. I paid $157 for my flight out of Dallas and $86.00 for my return flight home. You can't beat a round-trip plane ticket with no baggage fees for under $250.00.

When you go to book your flight, do your best to fly out on a weekday (not Monday) as well. You'll save more over flying Friday, Saturday, Sunday or Monday since those fares are usually higher. For more vacations, you will save more by waiting longer to buy your ticket. Obviously you don't want to wait until the day before you want to leave, but a month or six weeks out seems to be the sweet spot for getting the best deal.

For holiday travel, however, it's reversed. Book your ticket as soon as you possibly can because the closer the calendar gets to the holiday, the higher your fare will likely be.

PLAN TO FILL UP

When you're planning a road trip, you need to plan your fuel stops. A lot of people don't realize that with the internet came a fantastic ability...to see gas prices in almost every city and state in the country. Sites like FuelEconomy.gov and have huge listings of places to find local gas prices by state. Gasbuddy.com is another popular one that even has an app you can download for while you're on the road. Knowing where the cheapest places on your route are to fill up can save you big bucks as you drive.

SKIP THE HOTEL

To save the most money on your vacation, you'll need to think outside of the box on lodging. If you're going to be gone overnight, why not think outside of the box on where you're sleeping? Do you absolutely **have** to sleep in a hotel? Again, I ask...at $100+ per night most places, do you absolutely *have* to sleep in a hotel? Instead of spending all of the extra cash you save, why not stay at a relative's house or crash in the bed of your truck or van (assuming that's what you have)?

Neither of those options work? How about camping somewhere? We often travel from Texas to Ohio to see my family which could get very expensive if I allowed it to. Instead of spending our nights at the local hotel, we take our tent and camping gear along and camp at a local state park. Instead of paying $115.00 a night for a hotel, we spend just $29.00 a night for a campsite using camping equipment that we already own.

SKIP THE SPENDING MONEY

Do you *really* need enough spending money that you could pay three of your bills? No. You don't. It's as plain and simple as that. While some spending money is great, if you allow for too much in your budget, you'll just end up overspending and bringing home a trunk load of useless souvenirs that will never see the light of day again. Instead, give each person a smaller set spending allowance and stick to it. There is no need for little Johnny to get everything he asks for and trust me, you don't need that "I was here…," "I ate at…," or "I saw the …" tee shirt. You wouldn't buy something like that that at home so why allow it on vacation?

Instead, make your own souvenirs. Take lots of photos and put together a scrapbook or collage when you get home. It is much cheaper and you'll have the added benefit of not bringing home a ton of clutter.

REPEAT AFTER ME: RESTAURANTS ARE BAD

Before you leave for the road, pack a cooler with food and drinks. There's no reason that the kids can't eat peanut butter and jelly sandwiches or a handful of trail mix on the road. Capri Sun makes a great and cheaper alternative to drinks on the way than stopping and buying a soda or bottled juice at every gas station. Pack a quick and light lunch and a few snacks for the road, stop at a nice rest stop (*daylight is best to be one hundred percent safe*) and then only stop once for a "real" dinner. Your budget will be happier and your family won't notice the change at all. Just be sure to bring enough trash bags to take care of the trash so it's not littering your car or the rest stops.

OPT FOR THE DISCOUNT

Places like CityPass and Entertainment.com both provide coupon books that can save you big not only on vacation, but locally as well. CityPass can save you on admission for quite a few different big ticket attractions if you're visiting a larger city and Entertainment's coupon books can save on food, hotels, attractions and so much more.

If you buy an Entertainment Book and don't use the entire thing, leave it behind for your friends and family to use if you went home for vacation or stash it in the hotel dresser. I guarantee you that someone will come along who can use it and you'll do a good deed by not letting the coupons go to waste and helping someone else to save a few dollars.

GO FOR FREE IF YOU CAN

As I mentioned in the gift section, there are a whole slew of websites, and I do mean a whole slew of them, that allow you to earn points in exchange for gift cards or cash. Make use of these sites when you're thinking of your family vacation. Right now, I'm currently working on Southwest Airlines gift cards from one of my favorites. Why?

Because I don't want to pay full price for 3 people the next time that I must fly. These sites can be used to help pay for a vacation by giving you gift cards (or cash) for food, lodging, gas and more. Each site has their own minimums required to cash out and each one will have their own length of time that they pay you but these can be a huge asset when planning a vacation or road trip on the cheap.

The Frequent Traveler

If you travel a lot as a family, you may want to consider other discount programs available to you. Good Sams is an RV club that can help you save on gas and there are other clubs that can save you as much as 75% on discounts at zoo's, museums and more. These aren't a great idea if you are only traveling once a year, but for those who are on the road a lot? They're worth it.

Check your Bank Rewards

Surprisingly, some banks offer member benefits that can help you save on vacation. For instance, as Bank of America customers we save on museum admissions without doing anything other than being their customer. Your bank may not offer anything of this nature, but it is certainly worth checking.

THE SMALL SAVINGS

The biggest thing that separates the thrifty from the truly frugal is the ability to recognize that any savings is a good savings. Something may only save you a few pennies, but those pennies add up to dollars and dollars add up to six figures if you have enough. Knowing that, why would you overlook those small opportunities to save?

SMALL SAVINGS IDEAS

- Use coupons to help you save, but use them wisely. Don't buy something just because you have a coupon and never shop with your coupon binder or carrier with you. You will almost always spend more if you do.
- Check unusual places for deals – I purchase a lot of groceries through Amazon. So many that my daughter thinks it's hilarious that I often get things like PowerAde in the mail. Walmart is another great online option to check as they will often mark things down online, but not in store.
- Use all savings apps you can find, but don't purchase an item just to get the cash back rebate.
- Reuse what you can – Things like freezer bags and tea bags can be used more than once with very little loss in quality. Hang tea bags or lay them on a cookie sheet to dry and reuse as you normally would a second time before tossing them. For baggies, wash, rinse and dry well then reuse like normal. For safeties sake, though, don't reuse bags that have held meat. There's too many potential dangers there.

- Take chicken breast, especially boneless skinless chicken breast off your grocery list and buy thighs instead. You'll save an average of $2.00/lb. off your grocery bill. Chicken thighs can be just as meaty and the bones make a fantastic chicken stock. If you absolutely must have breast meat? Buy from someplace like Zaycon Foods or buy it bone in with skin and do the deboning work yourself. You'll spend more over thighs, but you'll still save over buying boneless skinless pieces.
- Switch from old school lightbulbs to more energy efficient CFL bulbs.
- Turn the temperature of your water heater down.
- Turn the water heater completely off by flipping the breaker when you know you're not going to be needing hot water (such as during the day when everyone is at work or school). You won't waste the energy to keep the water hot when no one will need it.
- Shut off ceiling fans when no one is in the room. They don't do anything at all to cool your home when no one is sitting there.
- Make certain that your windows and doors are sealed properly so there are no air leaks. If you find leaks, use a can of Great Stuff (*yes, that is what it is called*) or plastic visqueen sheeting to cover or fill them.
- Double check that your attic is insulated correctly to help air (warm and cool) stay where it should be.
- Use a slow cooker or grill to cook during summer months. You won't cause your kitchen to heat up or cause the a/c to have to run harder. On the flip side, cook with your oven and stove in the winter. You'll

heat the kitchen up helping to keep your home warmer.

- If you have a room or two in your home that isn't being used, you're paying to heat (or cool) an unused room. Close the vents and shut the door. If you're worried about air seeping into the rest of the house from under the door, roll up a towel and place it in front of the crack at the bottom to block most of the air. (Most interior doors have at the very least a small crack at the bottom of them between the floor and the door.)
- Check the filter on your furnace - If your filter is nasty, it won't heat or cool as well as it could.
- Buy a programmable thermostat and a locked thermostat case to keep anyone from playing with the temperature.
- If you buy fabric softener sheets, there's no need to use the full sheet. There is plenty of softening ingredients in one half of the sheets so cut them in half to save. Instead of paying an average of $0.03 per sheet, you'll drop your cost down to around a penny each.
- Make anything and everything you can homemade.
- Brush your teeth. Brushing does more than just help you look pretty. It also helps you save money since diseases of the mouth and gum can have huge effects on the rest of your health which can be super expensive to treat.
- Make sure you drink plenty of water and get plenty of exercise. Again, being unhealthy is expensive.
- Grow a garden
- Learn to can and dehydrate foods.
- Make your own compost

- Switch to cloth diapers for babies.
- Switch to cloth pads for women (although not every woman will be comfortable with this) if you're comfortable or use a menstrual cup instead of paying for pads or tampons.
- Make birthday cakes at home
- Make homemade pizza instead of ordering out.
- Learn to bake bread
- Buy a reusable water bottle instead of buying throw away ones.

While these ideas won't save you thousands, they will help you save. This list isn't all inclusive, but they're a fantastic place to start, especially if you're new to cutting your expenses.

Small Actions Create Big Savings

When your budget is tight, it be frustrating and damaging to work at cutting your expenses but not be able to get them cut back far enough to make a difference. It's easy to completely overlook that you're spending money on something; especially if you're used to spending that money. I will be honest and admit that it has happened to me more than once. My friends and I laugh at how I am so budget conscious but I can also be pretty expense dense sometimes.

Wasteful expenses

Wasteful expenses are just that. They are expenses in your budget or home that cause you to waste money. In other words, they are expenses that should be cut out of your budget, especially when you think you have nothing left to cut out.

Here are a few ideas of some wasteful expenses:

Stop buying bagged ice. Period. Your freezer makes the same thing for a lot cheaper. If your fridge doesn't have an ice maker, ice cube trays are affordable.

If you've got men or boys in your life, chances are you're spending around twenty dollars every few weeks to cut their hair. Stop paying that money and instead, spend that twenty on a set of clippers.

Did you know that you can clean your windows and mirrors with rubbing alcohol or vinegar and some crumpled newspaper? It's cheap as all get out and works even better than the blue stuff.

Skip buying jarred pizza or pasta sauce and make your own. You just need tomato sauce, a bit of sugar and the right spices. Not only does it taste better, it's cheaper too.

Commercial air fresheners are full of chemicals that you're spraying into the air where your kids live. Instead, stash a dish filled with baking soda in various places of your home. The baking soda absorbs odors keeping them out of the air. Again, if you want a scent to be released, use an essential oil that you're fond of and give the dish a good stir every so often.

Paper towels aren't just bad for the environment, they're also horrible for your budget. Instead, consider switching to unpaper towels. We made the switch not too long ago and I don't have a single regret. I picked mine up on Etsy for around one dollar each (12 for $12.00) and they have already paid for themselves many times over.

Are you paying for a gym membership? Why? You have an outdoors near you I'm sure. 99% of us do. Use it instead. It's free.

Cable television is a HUGE waste of money and one that you can save by cancelling your cable and picking up Hulu Plus, Netflix or both.

Drop the expensive cell phone plan and go pre-paid. Boost Mobile is a great one but if you're looking to save, Republic Wireless is where it's at. The average bill for a Republic Wireless customer is $15.00/mo.

I'm sure you get the idea. Wasteful expenses need to be cut out of your budget almost as soon as you realize they are there. If not, they can eat away at your funds until you have very little to nothing left.

FAMILY BUDGET: CRISIS MODE

As much as we'd like to pretend it doesn't, sometimes it happens to the best of us. We're trotting along, working out jobs, paying our bills, buying groceries, paying for the kid's sports and clubs and everything is fine. Then suddenly, we wake up and BOOM! There's no money left, the bills aren't paid and there is way too much time left over before you'll be able to afford things again. It's a vicious cycle that once it starts, doesn't stop without help and can easily ruin your family's finances if you let it. When your family budget is in crisis mode, it's easy to get discouraged and depressed.

Let's face it; none of us like telling our kids that they can't do something or having to choose between what we normally have just so that we can make ends meet. It's necessary though if you're going to stand on a solid financial ground again though. The steps below will help you get out of budget crisis mode and will give you a running start towards fixing that crisis.

GET COMMITTED

So here's the thing…if you're trying to get out of trouble with your budget, it will require not only *you* personally to be committed, but your **entire** family as well. Whether you involve your kids will of course depend on their ages, but **every single adult** who has anything to do with your budget, **needs** to be committed to cutting expenses and saving money. If even one person is not, the entire thing will come crashing down on you and a lot of the time, the second crash is much worse than the first.

Determine Want vs. Need

This issue right here is where a lot of families run into trouble. In today's world, it is very easy to think you need something when you in fact don't. How many times as your child whined, "But Mom! I nnneeeeeeeed it!!" (Cue the puppy dog eyes and full on pouty lip here). Most of us as parents will tell them no and move on with our lives. The sad truth is though, *we're horrible about telling ourselves no.*

"But Stacy! I neeeeedddd that Starbucks coffee every morning!"

"I neeeeedddd that cable TV!" "I neeeeedddd that new purse"

Put your big girl (or boy) panties on because guess what? You don't.

In fact, you only have FOUR (4) basic needs. Everything else and I do mean everything...is a want. As of right this second, your needs are:

- Shelter
- Food
- Utilities
- Transportation

That's it! You must have food to survive, you have to have water to cook and bathe, electric to heat or cool by (and sometimes cook), trash pickup so your family doesn't get sick...you have to have a place to live and you have to have a way to get to and from work. It is that simple. Internet? Not a need. Cable TV? Not a Need. Cell Phone? Nope. Starbucks? Uh-huh. McDonald's for lunch every day? Not a chance.

To climb out of financial crisis mode, you must figure out your family's basic needs. New clothing is **not** a need right now for 99.9% of people. Chances are, your closet is already full of clothing. The exception to this would of course be babies and diapers, etc. School lunches are **not** considered a need to me. Your kids can pack and they won't be any worse for the wear for doing it. Even Little Johnny's karate classes are **not** a need. Johnny can wait to get his belt until the budget has a bit more play in it. It won't hurt him and he will learn a valuable lesson while waiting.

Sit down and figure out your needs and only your needs are and write them down with the amounts they are each month. You now know the very minimum amount your family needs to survive.

CUT THE WANTS

It can be painful sometimes to realize just how much we are be spending on things that we don't need. For a lot of folks, things add up and continue to add up until they just lose track of the amount of money they've spent on an item.

-Look at this:

If you spend $5.00 per day at Starbucks, 5 days a week that is $25.00 per week.

There are 4 weeks in a month so that is $100.00 a month spent.

There are 12 months in a year so that is $1200.00 a year spent at Starbucks and that isn't even accounting for when a month has 5 weeks!

I don't know about you, but that $1200.00 a year? That is a month's rent for my family. It is almost a year worth of electric bills. It is 2.5 years of water bills for us. It is 2 years of paying our phone bill. It is 18 months of car insurance for us. I would certainly rather throw that $1200 toward one of those things than I would a drink that I'm going to be able to enjoy for maybe 30 minutes of my day.

Now put that into perspective with your cable bill, Johnny's Karate classes, the extra cell line, your daily lunch at work and more. I would be more than willing to bet that you'll find hundreds of dollars, if not thousands, of your money just floating away.

In step 2, you labeled the items that were just needs for your family. Now, I want you to go cut absolutely everything that isn't on that list. Turn it off, shut it down for a few months, cancel it, or whatever it takes. If you cannot pay for your basic needs, you cannot have it. You can't afford to!

PAY THE BILLS AND SAVE

Once you've got your needs vs wants taken care of totally, it's time to pay what you can. Figure up how much money you have coming in for the rest of the month, if any. Start with your needs only. Pay each one on paper until there is no money left. If you can't pay them all, start moving money around until you can at least pay something to each one. Try not to skip *any* of them because frankly, it is better to make a partial payment on something than it is to make no payment at all.

When the first of the month rolls around, re-do your income and your expenses again (using only the basic needs again). Try to get everything caught up, especially if you only made partial payments the month before. If you have any income left over after everything is paid for, do **not** spend it.

That money- **any** extra money that you have left- needs to go into your savings account to slowly build your emergency fund back up and to create a buffer for yourself for the next month. Each month, you'll do this exact same thing. Each month you'll put that extra money into savings.

After a few months of doing it this way, you will be sitting in a better position and can take a second look at your budget to see if you can start adding those wants back in.

IF THERE'S NO WAY, MAKE ONE

If you are in a position where you absolutely cannot find the money to pay for your needs on a month to month basis, you **must** make one, even if that means getting help in some areas. SNAP benefits can help with food and a lot of communities have places that will help with rent or utility costs. In most communities, you can dial 211 from any landline to find out the location of these places and what you'll need to apply for their programs.

Getting a second job can help too and you can bring in money even if you're staying at home. In the next chapter, I give you a few ideas for boosting your income just in case you need a good place to start.

If you've done all those things and still can't find the cash, start selling the items that your family has but no longer needs or wants. Even things that they want, but will bring in cash can be sold as a last-ditch effort. There are very few items in our homes that are truly irreplaceable. We are just so conditioned to have more stuff than the guy next door that we think they are. Facebook has a ton of buy/sell groups, Craigslist is always an option, but please be safe if you're using it. Ebay is another option as well, but make it your last one because often the fees make it not worth it.

There is always a way and if after cutting everything you can and getting help, you are still having trouble? You'll just have to make that way yourself.

Boost Your Income

In the last chapter, I told you that if you can't pay your bills on your current income that you need to find a second (or third) job. This is especially important if your budget is currently in a crisis mode. There are a lot of things you can do to pick up some extra cash that don't involve selling everything you own.

Work from Home

Working from home is always a fantastic way to make money when you need it, but do be careful about which home based business idea you choose to go with. There are a lot of work at home companies out there but not all of them are honest.

Work at Home Business Ideas

If you're looking for ideas on how to create a work at home business, look at the list below and use them to make yourself some money or as a jumping off point for your own ideas.

- Cake baking and decorating
- Soap making
- Candle making
- Sewing
- Proofreading
- Freelance writing
- Daycare
- Start a blog – I have a tutorial on the Six Dollar Family blog that walks you through getting a blog going easily. You can find it here:

http://sixdollarfamily.com/how-to-start-a-blog-in-3-easy-steps

If you don't want to work from home, check your local want ads, Craigslist and more for places that you can take a second job with. Even if you just work a few hours a week, it will help you bring in a bit of extra income for your family.

WHY I DON'T RECOMMEND MOST NETWORK MARKETING

While there are people who have struck it rich with network marketing, the clear majority of people don't. The people who are have made the most are the people who started with the company on the ground floor. Instead, you often find people who pay a hundred dollars or more to buy their kit or starter pack, give it a good shot and end up quitting early on. All the while they're paying fifty, one hundred or more dollars each month for product and supply because they know they won't be paid if they don't.

I'm not saying that you can't make money with an MLM. I've got several friends who make very good money with an MLM. What I am saying though is to be very careful, go in with your eyes wide open and be absolute certain that your budget can handle the monthly expense.

I have found a couple (three to be exact) of exceptions to this rule, but in general, MLM programs that are worth it is few and very far in between.

Earning Extra Cash Online

I've mentioned them multiple times, but there is a very large amount of sites and apps that you can use online to earn a little bit of extra cash. In fact, I actually use several of these sites every day to add over two hundred dollars a month to my budget. It takes me less than an hour of active working and the rest is entirely passive. Don't overlook these sites even if you hate doing things like surveys. They could be your saving grace if you get into trouble with your budget.

Investing to Boost Your Income

Investments are a great way to bring in more income and to build your way to a six figure bank account, but keep in mind that there are many ways to invest. Before you get started, I highly advise that you do some research and learn about the different types of investments.

Ones that you'll want to look into are stocks, bonds and mutual funds. For those that want to pretty well automate things and aren't necessarily interested in building their investment portfolio quickly, the Acorns app is a good way to go. Mutual funds can also be a good place to start for those who want a hands off approach since they're managed by mangers instead of by you personally.

If you want to grow your savings balance but don't want to take the risk that investments can have, a money market account is a great option. Money market accounts work like savings accounts, but they generally have a higher interest rate. It's a great option for those who want to let their savings grow for a bit without taking too many withdraws.

CONTINUING YOUR JOURNEY

As I said in the first chapter of this book, frugal living is a lifestyle and one that some of you will just be starting. Living a life where you strive to save every penny can be a hard one, but it is one that given enough time and effort, will reward you greater than you could ever expect.

You are going to have days where you get discouraged. You're going to have moments where you wonder if it's all worth it. You're going to fall and you're going to fail and you're going to want to simply give up and to just stop saving. Spending is easier after all.

Don't.

If you give up, you will end up with what everyone else does; bills that are unpaid, kids that don't have the skills they need to support themselves, wasted time, wasted money and a mountain of debt.

If you keep on the journey though, you will find yourself with a comfortable life and a secure future for not only yourself, but you're helping to build habits that will help your kids in their lives as well.

When things get tough, remind yourself why you picked this book up in the first place...and then get right back at it.

MONEY SAVING RESOURCES

Throughout this book I have mentioned a lot of different sites and apps that can be used to help you save. To make it easier for you to help yourself with those resources, I've added the ones that I mentioned and a bunch of others to a page on my blog to help you save. Some are the sites that I've already mentioned and others were not mentioned here. Some are blog posts already on the Six Dollar Family blog, but that I did not add to this book. No matter though because combined they can help you save thousands big.

You won't want to miss this list though no matter what you do!

To view it, visit www.sixdollarfamily.com/big-ways-to-save

About The Author

Stacy Barr is the face and brain behind the frugal living and lifestyle blog Six Dollar Family. A true gypsy soul, her newest blog, Unsettled Hearts, chronicles the journey of her family to become full-time travelers. By the age of 30, Stacy had overcome an alcohol addiction, a drug addiction, divorce, survived domestic violence and had built a life for herself and her daughter after spending 10 months in a homeless shelter. She began blogging in 2008, became a professional blogger in 2011 and in 2015 published her first book. Stacy is available for guest posting, appearances and to teach financial/budgeting classes.

Learn more about Stacy at
http://www.sixdollarfamily.com.com/bio

Connect with Stacy on:

Facebook at http://facebook.com/SixDollarFamily

Pinterest at http://pinterest.com/SixDollarFamily

Twitter @SixDollarFamily

Instagram @ SixDollarFamily